365
GARDENING
HINTS AND TIPS

SUSAN MCCLURE, M.S.

C. COLSTON BURRELL, M.S., CONSULTANT

PUBLICATIONS INTERNATIONAL, LTD.

CONTRIBUTORS:

Susan McClure has an M.S. in botany and is the author of over a dozen gardening books including the *Herb Gardener* and *Culinary Gardens from Design to Palate*. She also writes for magazines and newspapers, teaches at the Chicago Botanic Garden and Morton Arboretum, and is a regional director of the Garden Writers of America.

C. Colston Burrell is a Master of Landscape Architecture and has an M.S. in horticulture. He is a garden designer, writer, consultant, and photographer, and is president of Native Landscape Design and Restoration, Ltd. He coauthored the *Illustrated Encyclopedia of Perennials*, contributed to the *New Encyclopedia of Organic Gardening* and *Landscaping with Nature*, and has served as consultant to many gardening books, including *Treasury of Gardening*.

Cover photo: **Heather Angel Photography**

Illustrations: **Marlene Hill Donnelly**

CONTENTS

❧ Contents ❧

INTRODUCTION

If you enjoy working in the yard and are thinking about starting a new garden or improving an existing landscape, you'll find a wide array of fun and easy projects in this book. *365 Gardening Hints and Tips* provides special tips on how to employ useful gardening tools and techniques for every element in your landscape. We'll give you information about new types of flowers and plants, many of which have been specifically bred to be more resistant to pests and diseases, and we'll also tell you about new methods of improving your garden. Many of the hints in this book only require everyday household items or a simple change in the way you're already gardening! Our goal is to make gardening easier and more fun while you're doing it so that it will be even more pleasurable once you're done.

Inside this book, you'll find a number of ways to make garden upkeep easier, like

letting snow serve as a winter mulch, allowing toads to tackle insect pests, or using a
perforated pipe to aerate your compost pile.
In *365 Gardening Hints and Tips,* you'll learn
surprisingly simple tricks of the trade, such
as using a clear plastic bag to make a miniature greenhouse, shaping the lawn so it's
easily mowed, and positioning warm-colored
flowers for increased impact in distant gardens.

   This book is divided into two sections.
The first section, "Gardening Basics," is all
about those elements of gardening that seem
so elementary, we may want to take them for
granted! But by focusing just a little extra
attention on fundamental things like soil,
water, and light, you can make a major difference in your garden. Perhaps you need to
do a soil test to determine if you should
adjust the nutrients in the dirt, or maybe you
need to switch the time of day that you're
watering your plants. Any extra time and
effort you spend in the garden early on will
ensure an even greater reward at bloom or

harvest time. We'll also discuss how to prevent pests and diseases from ruining your handiwork, how you can propagate your plants to increase your own supply or share with a friend, and how organic and low-maintenance gardening can add to the ease and enjoyment of this popular hobby.

The second section of the book, "Types of Gardens," focuses on the various elements included in the landscape, such as shade trees and evergreens, annual and perennial flowers, herbs and vegetables, and, of course, the lawn. Each part of the landscape is important, and we'll help you decide how to make the very most of your garden. We'll also give you hints about bulbs, roses, ground covers, and vines. Just because these elements may seem fancy doesn't mean you can't grow them beautifully—and easily! With a little planning and our helpful hints you can create a landscape filled with an abundance of flowers, trees, and greenery. Dig in!

GARDENING
BASICS

There are libraries full of how-to books that explain the things you *need* to know for an outstanding yard and garden. But this book goes beyond that, featuring hints and tips you'll *want* to know—those little extras that can make a big difference. You'll discover ways to do things better, easier, or faster with new products, new techniques, and new plants. The practical advice offered here will help you enhance the growth of your flowers, vegetables, herbs, and other plants—often with less work than you were doing before!

But even the best tips can't change the fundamentals of gardening. Most plants need good soil with suitable drainage, texture, and fertility. They need moisture, light, nutrients, and occasional pruning to keep them healthy and thriving. These basics provide an important foundation for any yard or garden, and with our helpful hints, you'll be sure to get started off right. The tips included here will help you enhance your landscape—and maybe even your enjoyment of gardening.

CHAPTER 1

THE DIRT ON SOIL

Children who are scolded for running into the house in dirty shoes may come to believe dirt is a bad thing. But just the opposite is true as long as dirt remains outdoors where it belongs. In the garden, dirt is transformed into soil, a complex and beautiful (at least to experienced gardeners) blend of animal, vegetable, and mineral material. Good soil is the first step to a great garden.

The loose, dark earth of fabulous gardens seen on television and in magazines doesn't usually just happen. It is created by gardeners improving their native soils. Soils can be amended with sand to make them looser and drier or with clay to make them moister and firmer. They can be given plentiful doses of organic material—old leaves,

9

ground-up twigs, rotted livestock manure, and old lawn clippings. Organic matter improves and nourishes any kind of soil, which, in turn, encourages better plant growth.

I — USE PLANTS ADAPTED TO THE CONDITIONS RIGHT OUTSIDE YOUR DOOR.

When plants prefer your native soil and climate, no matter how difficult these conditions may be, they are likely to grow beautifully with little effort. Native plants—shade trees, shrubs, or flowers that arise in the nearby countryside—are good options. Or, try less common plants from faraway places with conditions similar to your own.

To identify suitable plants, begin by identifying your garden conditions. Have your soil tested or do your own tests (see Hint 5) to determine if you have a light and sandy soil, a moderate and productive soil, or a heavy clay soil. Watch the site to see how sunny it is, and select plants that need full sun, partial sun, or shade, accordingly (see Hint 31).

Finally, check through nursery catalogues and gardening books to find plants that thrive in every one of the elements particular to your yard. Use these plants as a shopping list for all of your future gardening projects. A little extra legwork in the beginning makes gardening much easier over the coming years.

2 **GET A SOIL TEST** before you start adding fertilizers and amendments to your garden soil. This follows the old advice: "If it ain't broke, don't fix it." Sometimes unnecessary tampering with nutrients or soil acidity can actually create more problems than benefits.

Soil tests tell you the nutrient levels in your soil, a plant version of the nutrient

SOME SOURCES OF SPECIFIC NUTRIENTS

Many of these fertilizers are available processed and packaged. You don't have to harvest your own.

NITROGEN: livestock manure (composted), bat guano, chicken manure, fish emulsion, blood meal, kelp meal, cottonseed meal

PHOSPHORUS: bonemeal, rock phosphate, super phosphate

POTASSIUM: granite meal, sulfate of potash, greensand, wood ashes, seabird guano, shrimp shell meal

CALCIUM: bonemeal, limestone, eggshells, wood ashes, oyster shells, chelated calcium

BORON: manure, borax, chelated boron

COPPER: chelated copper

MAGNESIUM: Epsom salts, dolomitic limestone, chelated magnesium

SULFUR: sulfur, solubor, iron sulfate, zinc sulfate

ZINC: zinc sulfate, chelated zinc

IRON: chelated iron, iron sulfate

guides on packaged foods. They also note pH and organic content, two factors important to overall smooth sailing from the ground up.

To have your soil tested, call your local Cooperative Extension Service, often listed under federal or county government in the phone book. Ask them how to get a soil testing kit, which contains a soil collecting bag and instructions. Follow the directions precisely for accurate results.

The results may come as a chart full of numbers, which can be a little intimidating at first. But if you look carefully for the following, you can begin to interpret these numbers:

- ➷ If the percentage of organic matter is under 5 percent, the garden needs some extra compost.
- ➷ Nutrients will be listed separately, possibly in parts per million. Sometimes

they are also rated as available in high, medium, or low levels. If an element or two comes in on the low side, you'll want to add a fertilizer that replaces what's lacking.

🖎 Soil pH refers to the acidity of the soil. Ratings below 7 are acidic soils. From 6 to 7 are slightly acidic, the most fertile pH range. Above 7 is alkaline or basic soil, which can become infertile above pH 8. Excessively acidic and alkaline soils can be treated to make them more moderate and productive (see Hints 7 and 8).

3 | **ADD ONLY THE NUTRIENTS YOUR SOIL TEST SAYS ARE NECESSARY.**

More is not always better when it comes to plant nutrients. Don't feel compelled to add a little bit more of a fertilizer that promises great results. Too much of any one nutrient can actually produce toxic results, akin to diseases or worse. Buy only what's required and save the rest of your money for a better use, like more plants.

4 **LOOK FOR THE TALES WEEDS HAVE TO TELL** as they grow in your garden. Weeds are opportunists, taking advantage of any vacant soil to make their home. (Just think of how well this strategy has benefited the dandelion, a native of Eurasia that has swept through America.)

Although they seem to grow everywhere, dandelions prefer fertile, often heavy soil. Likewise, other weeds favor certain kinds of soil. For instance, acidic soil can encourage the growth of crabgrass, plantains, sheep sorrel, and horsetails. Alkaline soil (also called sweet or basic soil) is favored by chamomile and goosefoot. Fertile nearneutral soils can provide a nurturing environment for redroot pigweed, chickweed, dandelions, and wild mustard.

Even if you can't tell one weed from the other, you can find out important information by looking at them closely. If a vacant garden area has few weeds taking advantage of the opening, the soil is likely to need plenty of work. If they are growing, but only sparsely, and have short, stunted stems and discolored leaves, the area may have a nutrient deficiency, and a soil test is in order. If, in newly tilled soil, weeds sprout up quickly in certain areas and more slowly in others, the weedy areas are likely to be moister and better for seed germination.

5 **CHECK THE TEXTURE OF YOUR SOIL** in a jar filled with water. This test is simple to do at home and provides important information about your soil.

Gather up some soil from the garden,

choosing a sampling of soil from near the surface and down to a depth of 8 inches. Let it dry, pulverize it into fine granules, and mix well. Put a 1-inch layer (a little over a cup) in a quart glass jar with ¼ teaspoon of powdered dishwasher detergent. (Dishwasher detergent won't foam up.) Add enough water to fill the jar two-thirds full. Shake the jar for a minute, turning it upside down as needed to get all the soil off the  bottom, then put the jar on a counter where it can sit undisturbed.

One minute later, mark the level of settled particles on the jar with a crayon or wax pencil. This is sand. Set an alarm for 4 hours, and when it goes off, mark the next level, which is the amount of silt that has settled out. Over the next day or two, the clay will slowly settle out and allow you to take the final measurement. These measurements show the relative percentages of sand, silt, and clay, or the texture of your soil.

- Soil that has a high percentage of sand (70 percent or more) tends to be well aerated, ready to plant earlier in spring. But it also tends to need more frequent watering and fertilization than heavier soils.

- Soil that has 35 percent or more clay retains more moisture, so it takes longer to dry in spring and may need less watering in summer. It can be richer and more likely to produce lush growth with just the addition of compost and, occasionally, a little fertilizer. The compost is important. It helps break up clay so the soil won't be too thick and poorly aerated.

❧ Soil that has more equal percentages of sand, silt, and clay can have intermediate characteristics and is generally well suited for good gardening.

6 **TEST YOUR SOIL'S DRAINAGE** by digging a hole, filling it with water, and watching how quickly the water disappears. All the soil tests in the world won't do a better job than this simple project. It tells you how quickly moisture moves through the soil and whether the soil is likely to be excessively dry or very soggy—neither of which is ideal.

When it hasn't rained for a week or more and the soil is dry, dig several holes that are 1 foot deep and 2 feet wide. Fill them to the top with water and keep track of how long it takes for the holes to empty. Compare your findings to the following scale:

❧ 1 to 12 minutes: The soil is sharply

drained and likely to
be dry.

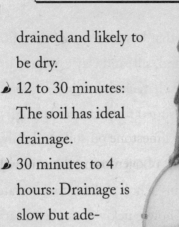

- 12 to 30 minutes:
  The soil has ideal
  drainage.
- 30 minutes to 4
  hours: Drainage is
  slow but ade-
  quate for
  plants that
  thrive in
  moist soil.
- Over 4 hours: Drainage is poor and
  needs help (see Hints 13 and 14).

7 USE GROUND LIMESTONE TO RAISE THE pH OF ACIDIC SOILS.

Limestone is nature's soil sweetener, capable
of neutralizing overly acidic soils. It's best to
add limestone in the fall to allow time for it
to begin to dissolve and do its job. The

20

amount of limestone you use will vary depending on the specific soil conditions. Simple home test kits, or a professional test, can be used to determine the soil's pH. If you dump limestone on soil randomly, you run the risk of overdosing the soil with lime. Follow guidelines on the limestone package or on a soil test.

Maintaining the new and improved pH is an ongoing project. Recheck the soil's pH every year and continue to add limestone as needed.

8 **TO LOWER THE ALKALINITY** and increase the fertility of limestone and other soils with very high pH, add cottonseed meal, sulfur, pine bark, compost, or pine needles. Garden sulfur is a reliable cure when added as recommended in a soil test. It acidifies the soil slowly as microbes convert the sulfur to sulfuric acid and other compounds. Soil amendments such as compost, decaying pine bark, and ground-up pine needles gradually acidify the soil while improving its texture.

9 **ADD A THICK LAYER OF MULCH** and let it rot to improve the soil of existing gardens. Minerals, released as the mulch is degraded into nutrient soup, soak down into the soil and fertilize existing plants. Humic acid, another product of decay, clumps together small particles of clay to make a lighter, fluffier soil. For best success, remember these points:

     🍂 Woody mulch such as shredded bark uses nitrogen as it decays. Apply extra

nitrogen to prevent the decay process
from consuming soil nitrogen that
plants need for growth.

🍂 Don't apply fine-textured mulches, like
grass clippings, in thick layers that can
mat down and smother the soil.

🍂 Use mulch, which helps keep the soil
moist, in well-drained areas that won't
become soggy or turn into breeding
grounds for plant-eating slugs and
snails.

10 **GET LOCAL COMPOST** from your
city or town hall service department.
Made from leaves and grass clippings collected as a public service, the compost may
be free or at least reasonably priced for local
residents. To find other large-scale com-
posters, check with the nearest Cooperative
Extension Service; they are up-to-date on
these matters. Or try landscapers and nurs-

eries, who may compost fall leaves or stable leftovers for their customers, and bulk soil dealers, who may sell straight compost or premium topsoil blended with compost. Don't give up. Yard scraps are discouraged or banned in many American landfills, so someone near you is composting them.

SOURCES OF ORGANIC MATTER

Compost
Livestock manure
Straw
Grass clippings
Salt hay
Shredded bark
Bark chunks
Shredded leaves
Seedless weeds
Peat moss
Kitchen vegetable scraps
Mushroom compost
Agricultural remains such as
peanut hulls or ground corn cobs

II **PLAN AHEAD FOR BULKY ORGANIC SOIL AMENDMENTS—**

compost, manures, and leaves—that may be added by the wheelbarrow-load to improve the soil. This will raise the soil level, at least temporarily. As the organic matter decays, the soil level will lower.

- If soils rich in organic matter drop to expose the top of a newly planted shrub or tree roots, add more soil or organic matter to keep the roots well under cover.

- If your garden is beside a house or fence, keep the soil level low enough so it won't come in contact with wooden siding or fencing that isn't rot resistant.

❧ When planting
around existing
trees, shrubs, and
perennial flowers,
avoid covering the
crown—where
stems emerge
from the ground—
with organic mate-

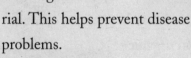

rial. This helps prevent disease
problems.

12 **DON'T WALK ON WET SOILS,**
especially clay soils. The footprints you
leave are evidence of compression—packing
the soil particles tightly and squeezing out
vital oxygen. This is not a desirable quality
in a garden. Put walkways or stepping stones
in the garden for easy access and to keep your
shoes clean and dry. When planting, cover
the soil with a board to kneel or stand on.

13 **TEST YOUR SOIL BY FEEL** before and after the soil is amended to judge the extent of the change. Take a small handful of lightly moist soil from several inches below the soil surface. Squeeze it into a ball in your hand and watch the results when you open your fingers. Sandy soils, which can have a scratchy feel, will fall apart. To enrich a sandy soil, apply a several-inch layer of compost and even an inch or two of clay, then try again. When the soil is improved, the ball will cling together better.

Clay soils, which have a slick feel, will form a tight ball that's not easily broken up. To lighten clay soil, add extra compost and coarse sand. When the soil is light enough, the ball will break up with a tap of a finger.

14 **TILL OR SPADE A THICK LAYER OF COMPOST** into lightly moist (never wet) soil to bring it to life before planting a new garden. The going may be rough at first if you are starting with hard, compacted soil. Use a rototiller and tough it out. Go over the area, removing weed roots and other underground vegetation as you go. Then go over the area again crosswise, until you break up the soil into reasonably small pieces. Your well-tilled soil, like screened topsoil, may look great at first, but silt or clay soils are likely to get stiff, crusty, and hard after a few heavy downpours. The best way to keep soil loose and light is to add organic matter.

Add a 4- to 6-inch-deep layer of compost to the soil and work it down until it's 10 to 12 inches deep. The soil will become darker, moister, and spongier—a dramatic conversion right before your eyes. As long as the organic matter remains in the soil, the soil is likely to stay loose. But since it slowly decays, you will have to continue to add organic matter—compost, mulch, or shredded leaves—in order to maintain the desired texture.

15 **TRY SPADING OR NO-TILL SYSTEMS TO PRESERVE THE TEXTURE AND ORGANIC CONTENT** of thriving garden soils. Once the soil is loose, light, and rich, minimal disturbance will help preserve the levels of organic matter. Avoid repeated tilling, which breaks healthy soil clumps and speeds up decay.

Instead of tilling, loosen rich soil before planting by turning the surface shallowly with a shovel and breaking it apart with a smack from the shovel backside. Very loose soil can be made ready to plant by combing it with a hoe or cultivator.

16 **DOUBLE-DIG GARDEN BEDS** to make high-performance gardens for deep-rooted plants like roses, a tradition in many beautiful English gardens. The average rototiller works the soil only 8 or 10 inches deep and won't break up compacted soil below. But double-digging will.

Double-digging requires of a bit of what the British call a stiff upper lip, because it takes a lot of manual labor. Do a little at a time so you don't overdo it, or hire a professional landscaper if you have health restrictions.

Start with vacant soil that is stripped of grass or other vegetation. Beginning at one end of the garden, remove a strip of soil

a spade's
length deep
and a
spade's
width wide.
Put it in a
wheelbarrow.
Use your shovel
to turn the soil
below it (likely to be one of the heaviest
parts of the job) and break it up. Another
(sometimes easier) option is to jab a garden
fork (like a big pitchfork) into the hard
lower soil and rock it around until the soil
breaks up. If organic matter is needed, you
should add it to the lower level at this point.

Do the same thing to the second strip
of soil next to the first row. But turn the
surface topsoil into the first trench, adding
organic matter as desired. Then loosen
and amend the exposed subsurface soil.

Continue filling each trench from the adjacent row and loosening the soil below. Fill the final strip with the soil from the wheelbarrow.

17 **BUILD RAISED BEDS** where the soil is too hard, rocky, poor, or wet for plants to grow well. Instead of struggling to change these bad conditions, construct a great garden bed over them. In vegetable gardens, simply mound up planting rows 6 to 8 inches high and 2 to 3 feet wide. (You can walk in the paths beside the planting rows without compressing the raised soil.) Permanent and decorative gardens can be set in handsome raised bed frames built of timbers, logs, rocks, or bricks and varying from 4 inches to 4 feet high. Don't hesitate to ask for professional help for big building projects, which need strong structures in order to last.

CHAPTER 2

THE WAYS OF WATER

At least 90 percent of every plant is composed of water, which should give you some idea of how important this substance is. No plant can live without some moisture, and certain plants use it in amazing ways. Orchids and bromeliads that live on tropical trees absorb rainwater through their foliage. Succulent plants and cacti store reservoirs of water in their swollen stem tissues so they can go for a month or more without rain. Prairie flowers such as butterfly weed store water in their fleshy taproots. And daffodils store water in their bulbs.

Without water, plants wilt and die. But too much water can be as bad for plants as not enough. If land plants are submerged in water for too long—even if just their roots are submerged—they may rot or drown from lack of oxygen.

Balancing plants' water needs is like having a healthful diet. Everything should be consumed in moderation. Provide your plants with enough water for good health, but don't flood them with it.

18 **APPLY WATER IN THE COOL OF THE MORNING OR EVENING** when the wind is calm, the sun is less hot, and water loss through evaporation is minimal.

19 **AVOID WATERING DISEASE-SUS-CEPTIBLE PLANTS AT NIGHT.** If water sits on plant foliage for hours, it can

PLANTS TO WATER IN THE MORNING, NOT AT NIGHT

Roses	Tomatoes
Apples	Cucumbers
Pears	Melons
Peaches	Beans
Plums	Begonias
Cherries	Geraniums
Grapes	Peonies
Strawberries	Dahlias
Raspberries	Chrysanthemums
Blackberries	

encourage fungal diseases to attack leaves, buds, flowers, and fruit. Plants susceptible to leaf spots, fruit rots, and flower blights are best watered in the morning, when the warming sun will quickly dry off the leaves and discourage fungus development.

20 **PROVIDE AN INCH OF WATER A WEEK** for many plants and lawn grasses. The idea is to keep the soil lightly moist and to prevent it from drying out completely, which would be damaging to most plants. But because plants don't always follow the rules, there are exceptions to this general guideline:

🌢 Hot weather, dry sandy soil, or crowded intensive plantings or containers may make more than an inch of water a week necessary.

🌢 When the weather is cool, the plants are widely spaced, or the soil is heavy and moisture-retentive, less water may be required.

🌢 Young or new plantings require more moisture at the soil surface to help their budding roots get started. You should water lightly and more frequently to accommodate their needs.

🌢 Mature plantings with large root systems can be watered heavily and less often than younger plants. The mois-

ture soaks deep into the soil and encourages the roots to thrive.

21 **SET A RAIN GAUGE IN AN OPEN
AREA OF THE GARDEN** to learn how
much water the garden receives each week.
You can purchase one at a garden center or
use a topless coffee can. After each rainfall,
check the depth of the rain inside. A commercial rain gauge is calibrated and easy to
read. To read rain levels in a coffee can, insert
a ruler and note how high the water has

come. Judge the
need for supple-
mental irrigation
accordingly (see
Hint 20).

Rain
gauges are also
helpful when
trying to deter-

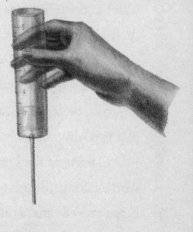

mine when you have watered enough with an overhead sprinkler. Since some sprinklers apply water unevenly (more up close and less farther out), you could set several rain gauges around the garden and compare the amount of moisture each one collects. If the readings vary widely, move the sprinkler more frequently or invest in a more efficient model.

22 USE GRAY WATER on potted plants or small gardens to reduce water use. Gray water is the leftover tap water from activities such as rinsing vegetables at the kitchen sink. However, avoid water contaminated with water-softener salts, harsh detergents, fats, oils, or other extras that would harm plants. Gray water has been used successfully in arid parts of the United States and is well worth taking advantage of anywhere. It helps prevent stress on wells during drought and lowers utility bills for people with municipal water lines.

Capture gray water in a basin stored close to the sink, where it will be handy to pull out and use. Transfer the gray water to a watering can before watering potted plants or new plantings. A little moisture in a time of need will make a big difference.

23 CATCH WATER FROM A DOWNSPOUT

into a container.
This unfluoridated,
unchlorinated water
is ideal for watering
plants. It comes at
an ambient temper-
ature, not shock-
ingly cold from the
tap—which is hard
on warmth-loving

plants. And perhaps best of all—at least from the gardener's perspective—it's free!

The easiest way to collect downspout runoff is to put a container at the bottom of the downspout. A topless bucket or barrel with a sturdy spigot at the bottom can be set in place permanently. Simply drain the water from the spigot into your watering can. To handle larger quantities of water, look for a 30- to 50-gallon barrel or drum. It's helpful to keep a large cup or other dipper on hand for transferring the water into a watering can.

You can tap every downspout around your house for maximum water yield or, if you prefer, just use the downspouts in the private parts of the landscape, the back and side yards.

24 **STRETCH SOAKER HOSES THROUGH THE GARDEN** to provide water directly on plant roots. Soaker hoses

are made of
water-per-
meable
fabrics,
perforated
recycled rub-
ber, or other porous
materials. When attached to
a hose with the water turned
on low or medium, moisture droplets weep
out along the length of the hose. Very little
evaporates and none sprays on plant foliage,
helping discourage diseases (see Hint 19).
But it may take an hour or more to moisten
nearby areas of the garden thoroughly.

Soaker hoses require a little special
attention in order to work properly. Here
are some hints:

🌱 Run soaker hoses through the garden.
   If turned or curved too sharply, they
   will kink and won't fill with water.

- Expect more water to be released from the end closest to the hose and less to be released from the far end.

- If the hose is moistening only one side of a plant root system, move the hose to water the dry side before you consider the job done.

- To determine if the soil has been watered enough, dig into the soil beside the hose. If the water has seeped 12 inches down, it's about time to turn the

MOISTURE-LOVING PLANTS

Louisiana and	Impatiens
Japanese irises	Hostas
Foamflowers	Ferns
Marsh marigolds	Joe-pye weed
Solomon's seal	Astilbes
Sweet flag	Umbrella plant
Horsetails	Ligularia
Swamp hibiscus	Mint
Chameleon plant	Cordgrass
Cardinal flower	Willows

hose off. Remember how long this took for the next time around.

🌢 For faster results, look for flat hoses that are peppered with small holes. Of course there's a trade-off: These hoses do provide water more quickly, but they are not as gentle on the soil.

🌢 If you like soaker hose results, you can upgrade to permanent or semi-permanent drip irrigation systems. Although more expensive, these systems are custom designed for varying soil types and individual plant water needs. They also don't require shuffling around the garden.

25 **WHEEL HOSE CARTS AROUND THE YARD** instead of dragging armloads of hoses and causing wear and tear on your back. Hose carts consist of a reel with a crank that you can use to neatly coil the hose, eliminating tangles, knots, and kinks. This reel is set on a two- or four-wheeled base with a handle for easy pulling. Look for large-wheeled types if you're rolling the cart over the lawn or rough ground. Smaller wheels are fine on a paved path or patio.

26 **PLACE HOSE GUIDES AT THE EDGES OF GARDEN BEDS** to keep the hose from crushing nearby plants when

you pull the hose taut. Hose guides, such as a wooden stake pounded into the ground at an outward angle, prevent the hose from sliding into the garden. More decorative hose

44

guides (stakes carved like decorative animals, elves, or flowers) can be found at some garden centers, mail-order garden suppliers, or craft shows. You could also improvise by using things like plastic pink flamingos, garden statues, or birdbaths.

27 SAVE WATERING TIME BY USING SELF-WATERING PATIO PLANTERS.

These pots aren't smart enough to turn on the faucet and water themselves, but they do have a lower-level moisture reservoir that's available to plants at any time. A wick, which may resemble fabric or rope, pulls the water up into the rooting area when the soil begins to get dry. Many different styles are available—and more kinds are becoming available every year. Another option is to buy a converter kit that turns regular planters into self-watering pots.

28 **USE A WATER BREAKER ON THE END OF YOUR HOSE** to change heavy water flow into a gentle sprinkle. This helps prevent soil compaction and spreads the water more evenly across planting areas. Put an adjustable spray nozzle on the end of the hose, watering only with the setting that produces fine droplets in a gentle spray and wide arc. Save the strong blasts for washing the car.

Or, look for spray heads developed specifically for garden use. Some are set on angled bases, making it easy to reach in between plants. Others are on long poles for watering hanging baskets.

Water breakers should be put on watering cans, too, especially when watering young plants such as seedlings, which can be broken or uprooted with a strong drenching.

29 **REDIRECT RUNOFF FROM DOWN-SPOUTS INTO FLOWER BEDS OR LAWN AREAS** to give plants extra water every time it rains. Flexible tubing could be connected to the end of the downspout and directed into nearby plant-ings around the foundation of the house or to flower or vegetable gardens. For maximum bene-fits, shape beds like a shallow bowl to collect the water and give it time to soak in. Or, as an alternative, the garden could be made fairly level with lower, moisture-gathering saucers made around newly planted trees or shrubs or plants with high moisture needs.

In dry climates, the tubing could be covered with soil or mulch and kept connected all the time. In climates with periods of overly wet weather, the tubing should be disconnected during soggy seasons to prevent oversaturation of the soil, which causes plants to rot.

30 **DROP THE SOIL LEVEL IN THE BOULEVARD STRIP,** the row of grass between the sidewalk and the street, so it will collect runoff rainwater that otherwise would be lost to street sewers or roadside ditches. A small 1- to 2-inch drop in soil level will be enough to do the job. If planting sod, make the soil level even lower to account for the extra height of sod roots. In cold climates, you may have to remove sand or grit that can accumulate after winter snowplowing to maintain an appropriate height.

CHAPTER 3

SHEDDING SOME LIGHT ON LIGHT

While sunshine may not literally make the world go 'round, it does power the process of photosynthesis, which makes many things possible. Photosynthesis allows plants to make their own food, using only air and water. As they grow, plants provide food for grazing animals who in turn provide sustenance for higher levels of the food chain. Since sun provides the start for the whole food pyramid, it's vital to give it the respect it deserves in the garden.

Many plants, especially lawn grass, flowers, roses, vegetables, fruit trees, and conifers (needle-leaved evergreens) thrive in bright sun, which provides abundant energy for growth, flowering, and fruiting. But some plants, particularly those native to forests and glens, need shadier conditions. Learn the sun requirements of any plant you intend to grow so you can put it in the right place.

31 **WATCH HOW SHADOWS AND SUNLIGHT HIT THE GROUND** to determine how much shade exists during the growing season under deciduous trees (which drop their leaves in fall). This test will determine which shade-loving plants will thrive there. Some suggested plants for varying degrees of shade are found in the list at right.

- Full shade is found under thickly branched trees or evergreens. A garden that's located here will receive little or no direct sun and remain gloomily lit. Only a limited number of plants are suitable for this situation. You should choose flowers and ferns with evergreen leaves.

❧ Partial shade can be found under trees
that allow sunlight to penetrate
through the canopy and dapple the

SOME PLANTS FOR SHADY CONDITIONS

PLANTS FOR FULL SHADE:
• Ferns, ivy, pachysandra, periwinkle

PLANTS FOR PARTIAL SHADE:
• Spring wildflowers: trout lilies, bloodroot, bellworts, Solomon's seal

• Shrubs: rhododendrons, azaleas

• Shade-loving perennials: bleeding heart, hostas, mint, bergenia, sweet woodruff, astilbes

• Annuals: impatiens, browallia

PLANTS FOR LIGHT SHADE:
• Annuals: begonias, coleus, ageratum, sweet alyssum

• Herbs: basil, parsley, bee balm

• Vegetables: lettuce, spinach, arugula

• Perennials: daylilies, hostas, anemones, hardy geraniums, coral bells, lobelia ground throughout the day. A garden grown under a lightly branched honey locust tree would fall into this category. A larger selection of plants are capable of growing under these conditions than in full shade.

❧ Light shade is found in places where plants are in direct sun for a portion of the day. This could be found in a garden under mature trees with long barren trunks. The sun can shine in under the high leaf canopies. Light-shade conditions also exist on the east or west side of a wall or building. Here you can grow many shade-loving plants as well as shade-tolerant plants, which are sunlovers capable of growing moderately well in light shade.

32 **GROW SUN-LOVING SPRING BULBS AND WILDFLOWERS** beneath deciduous shade trees to make the most of the sun before the tree leaves emerge. This is a great strategy for people who have a shady yard and therefore have trouble getting flowers to grow during summer and fall. Crocuses, squills, Spanish bluebells, daffodils, windflowers, glory-of-the-snow, and wildflowers such as bloodroot, squirrel corn, and other local natives thrive in spring sun. When tree leaves emerge and the setting grows dark, many of these spring growers fall dormant and lie quietly below the ground until spring sun arrives again.

33 **PAINT A DARK WALL WHITE** to reflect more light onto plants. Just like the silver solar reflectors used by sunbathers to intensify their tans, a light-colored wall will reflect additional light onto nearby plants. Similarly, using a mulch of white pebbles, sand, or gravel will reflect light up through the bottom of plants, a technique often used in gardens of Mediterranean herbs or silver-leaved plants that thrive on plenty of sun.

34 **LIMB-UP TREES** or remove smaller, scraggly, or unwanted saplings and brush to brighten a densely shaded spot. Tall, mature shade trees can have their lower limbs removed (a heavy job requiring a professional arborist) to produce light shade (see Hint 31). For even more light, arborists can thin out overcrowded branches in the

canopy, leaving some openings in the foliage for sun penetration.

Removing unwanted tangles of young trees, wild shrubs, and other woody growth is a project you can do yourself. Look for self-sown seedlings around trees such as maples, oaks, ashes, and elms. Crabapples will send up vertical sprouts called suckers, turning the tree into a bush. Get a pair of long-handled pruning loppers to trim out the smaller growth and a pruning saw to remove larger trunks. When finished, you can admire the newly revealed shape of the tree trunk and the ferns, hostas, and other shade plants that can grow beneath it. Be sure not to overthin; you should leave enough saplings to replace older trees as they die.

35 **PRUNE LOW-HANGING BRANCHES ON A SUNNY DAY** so you can see how the light changes. This way you can watch

the shade lighten.
You also can
keep an eye on
the shadows,
which will
dance from
one side of
the tree to
the other,
changing
with the time

of day and position of the sun. Their silhou-
ettes can be a beautiful part of the garden,
especially in winter when the dark shadows
stand out on the white snow.

36 **DO NOT PRUNE OAKS IN SUMMER.**
Even though this may be when you are
anxious to lighten shade the most, it will
make your trees susceptible to oak wilt disease. Prune, instead, in late winter.

37 **CONSIDER DIFFERENCES IN SUN INTENSITY WHEN PLANTING ON THE EAST AND WEST SIDE** of shade-casting trees or buildings. Even if east- and west-facing sites receive the same number of hours of sun, they will not produce identical results.

- Gardens with an eastern exposure are illuminated with cool morning sun, then shaded in the afternoon. They are ideal locations for minimizing heat stress in southern climates or for plants such as rhododendrons that can burn in hot sun.

- Gardens with western exposure are shaded in the morning and drenched in hot sun in the afternoon. Sunburn, bleaching, and sometimes death of delicate leaves can result, especially in warm climates and when growing sensitive young or shade-loving plants.

Afternoon sun can also cause brightly colored flowers to fade. However, the west side of a building is the ideal place for sun-loving plants.

SOME PLANTS FOR SUNNY CONDITIONS

EVERGREENS: boxwood, junipers, false cypress, yews, arborvitae

CONIFERS: pines, spruces, firs

TREES: maples, oaks, elms, magnolias, crabapples, hawthorns, apples, pears, peaches, plums

SHRUBS: roses, barberries, potentilla, spirea, lilacs

PERENNIALS: yarrow, sea thrift, Shasta daisies, chrysanthemums, coreopsis, pinks, coneflowers, blanketflowers

ANNUALS: portulaca, gazania, gerbera, marigolds, zinnias, dahlias

HERBS: lavender, astilbes, thyme, sage, rosemary

38 **TRY EXPOSING FLOWERING SHADE PLANTS TO A HALF DAY OF MORNING SUN** to encourage better blooming. Extra light can also keep the plants more compact, tidy, and self-supporting.

39 **PROVIDING 6 TO 8 HOURS OF DIRECT SUN A DAY** is sufficient for most plants that need full sun. The term "full sun" doesn't actually mean plants must be in bright light every moment of the day, only most of the day. The 6 to 8 hour minimum must be met, however, even during the shorter days of spring and fall for perennials, trees, and shrubs.

40 **WHEN GROWING POTTED PLANTS INDOORS,** supplement natural light with fluorescent or grow lights. Sometimes in winter the weather may be cloudy for days, even weeks. This creates problems for tropical plants, potted flowers, and even foliage plants that need light to remain healthy.

The solution is to hang a fluorescent shop light directly over your indoor plants. Special grow lights or full spectrum bulbs (formulated to produce light wavelengths that plants need most) can be used in place of fluorescent bulbs for spectacular results with flowering plants. For extra-easy maintenance, plug the lights into an automatic timer, then set them to turn on for 14 to 16 hours a day and off again at night.

CHAPTER 4

MAINTENANCE AND PRUNING

Like playing a lively game of tennis, keeping your garden looking great depends on having the right equipment, developing a good technique, and being organized enough to do the right things at the right time. This may sound like a lot to juggle, but once you understand the basics, it's easy.

For a start, you need good hoes, spades, rakes, pruners, and a sturdy wheelbarrow. Then you need to learn how to control weeds with cultivation and mulch (Hints 48 and 49). A few basic pruning cuts will help you rejuvenate and control the size of your shrubs and trees (Hints 50 to 55). Other helpful suggestions in this section will help you polish up the rest of the landscape.

Watch the calendar and note the dates things need to be done in advance. This lets you encourage desirable plant growth and deter difficulties before they happen, thereby keeping your maintenance chores to a minimum.

41 **PILE DUG-OUT EARTH ON A TARP** instead of on the grass when digging a hole for planting or excavating a garden pool. You can easily drag away any excess soil, and you won't have to rake up little clods trapped in the turf. Don't waste that soil. You can use it to build a waterfall beside the pool or to fill a raised bed for herbs or vegetables.

42 **BUY THE BEST TOOLS** you can afford. There is no substitute for good tools. Tools that cost half the price but last only two years (instead of 22 years) are not cost-effective in the long run. They may also fail you in the middle of a big project, just when you need them most.

One way to ensure good quality is to buy tools from a reputable dealer willing to guarantee their performance. For another quality test, look at the way tools are made. Tools with steel blades are strong enough to last for years without bending. Stainless steel is even better, because it won't rust. Spades, shovels, and forks with hard ash handles are unlikely to splinter or break in the middle of a heavy operation. People with smaller builds can find specially designed tools with smaller blades and shorter handles, which are easier to control than oversized tools.

43 KEEP HAND TOOLS IN A BASKET

on the garage or pantry shelf so they are always easy to find. Nothing is more frustrating than seeing a branch in need of a quick trim but having to search all over the house and garage for a pair of pruning shears. If all your tools are kept together—and returned to their proper basket after each use—simple garden projects will stay quick and uncomplicated.

44   **USE WIRE GRID SUPPORTS** instead of individual stakes to easily hold up bushy but floppy perennials such as peonies. You can buy commercial grid supports, which are handsome round or square grids

---

PERENNIALS THAT OFTEN NEED SUPPORT

Shasta daisies
Asters
Bellflowers (taller types)
Garden phlox
Pyrethrum daisies
Yarrows
Balloon flowers
Sedums (taller types)
Hollyhock
Foxglove

---

neatly set on legs; green grids are more cam-
ouflaged amid the foliage than metallic
grids. Or you can make your own grid supports out of a sheet of wire mesh, cut a little
wider than the plant it will support. The
extra length can be bent into legs.

The supporting
process takes one sim-
ple step. Set the grid
over a newly emerging
perennial in spring.
The stems will grow up
through it, retaining
their natural shape
while staying firmly upright.

The alternative (which occurs when you
let the plant sprawl before staking it) is more
difficult and less attractive. Corsetting the
drooping limbs with twine and hoisting them
up with a stake of wood can result in broken
stems and a miserable-looking specimen.

45 **ALWAYS SET HOES, SOIL RAKES, AND OTHER TOOLS WITH HORIZONTAL TEETH OR BLADES FACE DOWN** on the ground when not being used. If stepped on, the teeth or blades sink harmlessly into the soil. But if left upright, an unwary walker might step on the teeth, making the tool tip and the handle spring up into his or her face. This hurts!

For an even more organized approach, attach a topless and bottomless coffee can or similarly shaped plastic container to a fence post, securing it with wire. You can slip in the handles of rakes, shovels, and hoes, keeping them together, upright, and out from underfoot.

46 **KEEP A BUCKET OF CLEAN SAND AND MACHINE OIL** in the garage to cure tools after each use. This is particularly helpful for rust-prone digging instruments such as shovels, garden forks, and hoes. After use, rinse with water and dry the blades. Then insert them in the oil/sand mixture. The sand will scour off debris, and the oil will coat the metal, retarding rust.

Keep the tools together in one place, preferably close to your basket of hand tools (see Hint 43) so they will be easy to find when needed.

47 **USE A SHARP HOE TO CUT OFF WEEDS,** especially annuals, instead of stooping and pulling them. Using a hoe is quicker and easier than hand-weeding, plus it does a superb job. If you catch weeds when they are young seedlings, a single swipe will be all it takes to eliminate them. If they are older, cut them down before they go to seed to prevent future generations of weeds.

Perennial weeds such as dandelions may have large underground roots that will resprout after hoeing. You can keep hoeing in hopes of wearing them down. Or, as a faster alternative, when the soil is moist, use a corner of the hoe blade to dig down and help you loosen the root, then pull it up by hand.

When the hoe blade begins to get dull and takes more effort to use, sharpen it like a knife with a sharpening stone.

48 COVER GARDEN BEDS WITH A LAYER OF MULCH to keep weeds down and reduce the need for water. Annual weed seeds are less likely to sprout when the soil is covered with enough mulch to keep the soil surface in the dark.

When it comes to water, even a thin layer of mulch—nature's moisturizer—will reduce evaporation from the soil surface. Thicker mulches can reduce water use by as much as 50 percent.

Mulches vary in their appearance, makeup, and texture, which will influence how you use them. Here are some examples:

🍂 Varying appearances: For a soothing, natural-looking garden, use dark-colored organic mulches made of bark or compost. For a brilliant-looking garden, consider a mulch of bright gravel. In utilitarian gardens like a vegetable garden, plastic or straw makes an excellent mulch.

🍂 Soil improvement:

This calls for the use of organic
mulches that break down to add organic matter to the soil (see Hint 9).

🌶 Texture: For maximum effectiveness
with only a thin mulch layer, look for
fine-textured mulches such as twice-
shredded bark, compost, or cocoa hulls.
For an airy mulch, try thicker layers of
coarse-textured mulches such as straw
or bark chunks.

49 KILL OFF SOD OR DENSE WEEDS

by layering newspaper, compost, and
mulch directly on the garden site. This treatment cuts off the sunlight to unwanted
vegetation, which will eventually decay and
add organic matter to the garden. The newspaper decomposes, too. (What a bargain!)

If you build the compost layer at least
4 inches high, you can plant shallow-rooted
annuals or vegetable seedlings into it. In a

year or so, loosen the soil deeply or build it up into a raised bed if you want to grow deeper-rooted perennials, shrubs, and trees.

50 PRUNE WITH TOP-QUALITY PRUNING SHEARS, LOPPERS, AND A SAW.

Sharp blades and sturdy handles make pruning a breeze. Dull blades—rusty and sticking—make projects harder than they need to be. They can also cause wood to be crushed or torn, which is damaging to the plant. Look for hard, durable blades capable of being resharpened and a sturdy, smoothly operating nut holding the blades together. Hand shears should also have a safety latch to keep the blades closed when not in use.

Hand pruning shears are used for small stems under about a half-inch in diameter. Look for scissor-type blades, which make sharper, cleaner cuts than the anvil type with a sharp blade pressing on a flat blade. Also check out new ergonomically designed pruning shears that minimize repetitive motion stress.

Loppers are long-handled pruning shears with larger blades for cutting branches up to about 1¹/₂ inches in diameter. Pruning is easier if you buy a model with ratcheting action for more power with less effort.

Pruning saws should have narrow blades, be easy to maneuver into tight spaces, and be toothed on one side only.

51 **CANDLE-PRUNE PINES TO CONTROL THEIR SIZE** or make them branch more thickly. Candle-pruning (also called candling) refers to manipulating the candle-shaped new shoots that arise in spring. Before the needles enlarge, use your pruning shears to cut off a little, half, or most of the soft candle, depending on how

much you want
to limit size.
The cut
should slant
at an angle
instead of slicing straight
across the candle. Come the following
spring, clusters of new side branches will
appear. Continue candling each year for
more dramatic results.

Candling is especially handy for keeping mugo pines small enough for use near
the house or in a mixed border. It also can
help lanky, open-branched pines fill in to
form a more solid and substantial cone.

52 **RENEWAL-PRUNE FLOWERING
SHRUBS** by removing one-third of the
stems once each year. This modest effort
acts like a fountain of youth, keeping these
shrubs young. It's much better than shear-

ing, which reduces flowering, has to be repeated frequently, and can even accelerate aging.

Use pruning loppers or a pruning saw to cut the oldest stems off at the ground, ideally in early spring before the shrubs break dormancy. This timing encourages quick renewal, but a few spring flowers will be sacrificed on early bloomers. If you can't bear that thought, wait to prune until after flowering. As spring and summer progress, new branches will take the place of the old branches. If pruned every year, the shrub will

SPRING BLOOMING SHRUBS

Azaleas
Flowering quince
Cotoneasters
Forsythia
Fothergilla
Japanese kerria
Rhododendrons
Pussy willows
Lilacs
Viburnums

---

be continually rejuvenated, remaining
healthy and beautiful.

53 REJUVENATE TIRED, OVERGROWN,
OR WEAK SHRUBS by cutting them to
the ground. Although this may sound like
giving up, just the opposite is true. It can be
the start of a whole new shrub. This technique works well with easy-growing shrubs
such as lilacs, viburnums, butterfly bushes,

and boxwoods but is generally not effective with evergreen shrubs (except boxwoods).

The idea is similar to renewal-pruning, only more radical. It should be done in early spring before leaves or flowers emerge. Shrubs with strong root systems will re-sprout with a fountain of new stems. So that they don't crowd each other out, you should thin out excessively thick clumps to allow the strongest to continue growing and form the foundation for the new shrub.

Shrubs with weak root systems or dis-ease problems may not resprout. If there are no signs of life a month or two after cutting the shrub back, start looking for a replace-ment plant.

54 **PRUNE TO THE OUTSIDE OF A TREE'S BRANCH COLLAR** for fast healing and good tree health. The branch collar is the swelling located at the base of

the branch, where it arises from another limb or the trunk. The branch collar is like a hospital isolation ward; it houses protective chemicals that help keep diseases from invading the parent limb. When removing a branch for any reason, leaving that branch collar in place shuts out any passing pathogens.

55

SLANT PRUNING CUTS AWAY FROM THE BUD to encourage water to run off. This helps keep the bud healthy so it can grow and prosper.

56 **USE A LAWN MOWER EQUIPPED WITH A BAGGER** when you mow the grass and any fallen leaves in autumn. The mower will begin to shred up the leaves and mix them with the grass. This does twice the good of ordinary mowing: It saves you from raking, and the blended leaves and grass clippings are a dynamite combination for making compost. Empty the mower bag in an out-of-the-way place to make a compost pile. Use a garden fork to fluff the pile occasionally during winter, and you could have great compost by spring or summer.

57 **GROW A PLANT FOR AT LEAST TWO OR THREE YEARS** before you decide to remove it. It can take that long for a perennial plant to get comfortable in a new home and begin to really show what it can do. Allowing a trial period of several years also lets the plant get beyond setbacks from

difficult weather—slow growth after an
exceptionally cold winter or poor flowering
during a long drought, for instance.

58 **DON'T ASSUME YOU CAN'T GROW
A PLANT** if it dies once. If you like that
plant and are willing to buy another one, put
it in a different place—one better suited for
its light and soil needs.

59 **MULCH NEW PLANTS WITH
STRAW OR CHOPPED LEAVES
AFTER PLANTING IN THE FALL** to prevent root damage during winter. A little
mulch used immediately after planting can
help to keep the soil moist and encourage
continued root growth.

But the main reason to mulch lies
ahead in winter. Alternately freezing and
thawing, expanding and contracting soil can
break new roots or even push new plantings

out of the ground, a process called soil heaving. By mulching generously with an airy material like straw when the soil first freezes, you can help keep the soil frozen until winter ends, at which point the mulch can be removed.

60 **IN WINTER, MULCH EVERGREEN PERENNIALS AND GROUND COVERS WITH EVERGREEN BOUGHS** to protect them from winter burn (the cold-weather opposite of sunburn). When the soil is frozen, the wind is strong, and the sun is bright, moisture is pulled out of the vulnera-

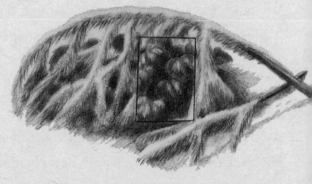

ble leaves and cannot be replaced by the frozen roots. A protective layer of evergreen boughs, possibly obtained by recycling the branches of a Christmas tree, forms a protective shield over vulnerable greenery. Straw will also do the job, especially in colder areas where there is less chance of rot in winter.

61 **CELEBRATE IF YOU LIVE IN A SNOWY AREA.** Snow is the best mulch of all, and it may allow you to grow plants that won't survive winter in snowless areas farther south.

CHAPTER 5

LOW-MAINTENANCE GARDENING

I f you are used to cutting your lawn every week and shearing your shrubs once a month, you may be relieved to know that there are easier ways to keep your yard looking nice. Low-maintenance gardening begins with choosing plants ideally suited for your yard's conditions so they won't need coaxing to stay alive.

Beyond that, some plants are naturally easier to keep, requiring little but suitable soil and sun exposure to grow and prosper. You can plant them and let them be without worrying about pests and diseases or extensive pruning, watering, fertilizing, or staking. Spending a little time finding these easy-care plants will prevent hours of maintenance in coming years.

Selecting the right style of planting for any given area can also reduce maintenance.

Instead of lawn grass that needs regular fertilizing, watering, and mowing, a self-sustaining meadow area can be appealing and leave you with plenty of time for your other interests. Or grow dwarf shrubs that don't need pruning for a trouble-free planting next to the house. These and other tips will help your landscape look great with less effort.

62 **CHOOSE DWARF AND SLOW-GROWING PLANTS** to eliminate the need for pruning and pinching. Tall shrubs just keep growing, and growing, and growing...sometimes getting too big for their place in the landscape. Lilacs, for example, commonly grow to 12 feet high. If planted by the house, they could cut off the view from the window. The only solution is regular trimming or replacement. A better option is to grow dwarf shrubs or special compact varieties that will only grow 2 to 4 feet high.

They may never need pruning and won't have to be sheared into artificial globes.

Tall flowers and vegetables may not be able to support the weight of their flowers and fruit. They might need staking, caging, or support with a wire grid (see Hint 44) to

COMPACT SHRUBS FOR FOUNDATION PLANTINGS

Dwarf balsam fir	Compact junipers
Compact azaleas	Leucothoe
Compact barberries	Mahonia
Compact boxwood	Dwarf Korean lilac
Heather	Dwarf spruce
Compact false cypress	Japanese andromeda
Cotoneasters	Mugo and other small pines
Daphne	Potentilla
Deutzia	Pyracantha
Fothergilla	Roses
Hydrangea, French and oakleaf	Spirea
Hypericum	Stephanandra
Compact hollies	Compact viburnums

keep them from falling flat on their faces.
Flowers such as delphiniums, asters, and
Shasta daisies are now available in compact
sizes that are self-supporting. And shorter
types of daylilies are less likely to become
floppy in light shade than taller types.
Compact peas and tomatoes, while not entirely
self-supporting, can be allowed to grow loosely
on their own, or they may need only small
cages or supports to be held securely upright.

63 **PLANT WEEDY SPOTS WITH
THICK-GROWING GROUND COVER**
to avoid becoming a drudge to weeding.
Ground cover works well on banks, in sun or
shade, under fencing where it's hard to keep
weeds down, beside outbuildings, and even
under trees where it's too shady for grass to
grow.

It's important to start the ground-cover
bed in weed-free soil, however, so the

ground cover can take over without competition. One easy way to get started is discussed in Hint 49. Another option is to clean up the soil. Turn it over with a rototiller or spade, let the weeds sprout, and then turn it again. Repeat the process until the weeds are almost gone.

Choose a ground cover that will thrive in the site. It needs to spread vigorously and grow thickly enough to crowd out any weeds that may try to work their way in. In shady areas, try ivy, pachysandra, barrenwort, wild ginger, or periwinkle. In sun, try creeping junipers, daylilies, ground cover roses, or other plants that are specifically suited for your climate.

For good results fast, buy plenty of plants and space them relatively close together. If this is too expensive, spread plants farther apart, and mulch the open areas to discourage weeds. Plan to keep a close eye on the new garden for the first year and pull up or hoe down any weeds that appear. Water and fertilize as needed to get the ground cover plants growing and spreading quickly. Once they've covered the soil solidly, there won't be any space for weeds.

64 **AVOID FAST-SPREADING AND AGGRESSIVE PERENNIALS** such as yarrow, plume poppy, 'Silver King' artemisia, and bee balm. Although these plants are lovely, they have creeping stems that can spread through the garden, conquering more and more space and arising in the middle of neighboring plants. Keeping them contained in their own place requires dividing—digging up the plants and splitting them into smaller pieces for replanting. This may need to be done as often as once a year. It's better to just avoid them.

65 **AVOID DELICATE PLANTS** such as delphiniums, garden phlox, and hollyhocks, which need extra care and staking. Although spectacular in bloom, these prima donnas require constant protection from pests and diseases, plus pampered, rich, moist soil and, often, staking to keep them from falling over. If you simply have to try one, look for compact and/or disease-resistant cultivars, which are easier to care for.

66 **IN AREAS DISTANT FROM THE HOUSE, PLANT NATIVE MEADOW GRASSES AND FLOWERS** that only need to be mowed once a year. Then have fun watching meadow garden flowers come and go throughout the season.

SOME MEADOW PLANTS

Black-eyed Susan	Snow-in-Summer
Dame's rocket	Butterfly flower
Evening primrose	Maiden pinks
Coreopsis	Penstemon
Blanketflower	Rock cress
Asters	Wild lupine
Coneflowers	Gayfeather
Shasta daisies	

You can find seed mixes or prestarted turflike carpets of meadow plants specially blended for different regions of the country. To feature your location's unique meadow plants, just let the area grow wild, and meadow plants will come on their own. (Be sure to explain what you are doing to your neighbors so they won't think your lawn-mower is broken!)

While they are getting started, newly planted meadows will need weeding and watering. Once in the late fall, after the flowers and grasses have all set seed, mow them down and let the seeds scatter to come up next year. Purchased wildflower carpets and mixes may contain colorful flowers that disappear after several years. You can sprinkle new seeds or plug in new clumps of a wildflower carpet to reintroduce them for color if you want.

67 MOW DOWN OLD FLOWER STALKS IN LATE FALL to clean up a flower garden. Before mowing anything but grass with your mower, make sure it has a safety feature that will prevent debris from being thrown out at you. Using suitable lawn mowers can save you plenty of time compared with cutting back the flower stalks by hand. If you allow the old stems to scatter around the garden, instead of bagging them, you may find an abundance of self-sown seedlings arising in springtime.

68 **BUILD GARDEN PATHS** anywhere that gets enough foot traffic to wear out the grass. Paths make pleasant straight or curving lines through the yard and make it easier to get where you need to go in wet weather. They also save you the trouble of having to constantly reseed barren, footworn areas.

Paths are useful else-where too. A path in the middle of a wide garden gives you access without having to walk through the soil. A narrow path can run along the front of a garden, serving as an edging, making the garden look neat, and keeping the grass out.

At its simplest, a path can be made with a surfacing of mulch or gravel. More elaborate paths can be made from stone, brick, or pavers.

69 **TURN A LOW, MOIST SPOT INTO A BOG GARDEN** for plants that need extra moisture. You can even excavate down a little to create a natural pond. Plant the moist banks with variegated cattails, sagittaria, bog primroses, marsh marigolds, and other moisture-loving plants. See the list on page 42 for additional plants.

70 **SPEED UP THE COMPOST-MAKING PROCESS** by chopping up leaves and twigs before putting them on the compost pile. The smaller the pieces are, the faster they will decay. Chopping can be easily done with a chipper-shredder or a mulching mower.

CHAPTER 6

ORGANIC GARDENING TECHNIQUES

Organic gardening is popular today, and for good reason: It works wonderfully! Organic gardeners shun the use of synthetic chemicals to keep their yards free from potential hazards. But the real success of organic gardens lies in the methods used to keep plants growing vigorously without a heavy reliance on sprays. Organic gardening cuts right to the heart of the matter: soil.

Soil is the life force of the garden. When enriched with organic matter, the soil becomes moist, fertile, and airy—ideal for healthy plants. It also nourishes a rich population of beneficial organisms such as earthworms and nutrient-releasing bacteria. And it harbors root-extending fungi that help make growing conditions optimal.

Organic gardeners also stress problem prevention in the garden. Putting plants in the right amount of sun, along with suitable soil, proper spacing, and ideal planting and watering, allows most plants to thrive with minimal upsets.

71 **MAKE COMPOST THE LAZY WAY** by layering leaves, lawn clippings, and kitchen waste. Then simply leave it until it's ready. Nature's recyclers will take organic matter no matter how it is presented and turn it into rich, dark compost. This process just takes longer in an untended pile.

To begin your compost heap, dump yard scraps in a far corner of the yard. An ideal blend would

be equal amounts of soft or green material
(manure and fresh leaves) and brown or hard
material (dead leaves and chopped twigs);
see the list on page 99. Or, if you prefer, keep
the compost materials neatly contained in a
wooden slat or wire mesh bin. If you put an
access door on the bottom of the bin, you
can scoop out the finished compost at the
bottom while the rest is still decaying.

72 **ADD COMPOST STARTER** or good
garden soil to a new compost pile
to help jump-start the decay of organic
materials.

Compost starter, available in garden
centers or from mail-order garden catalogues,
contains decay-causing microorganisms.
Some brands also contain nutrients, enzymes,
hormones, and other stimulants that help
decomposers work as fast as possible. Special
formulations can be particularly helpful for

hard-to-compost, woody material-like chips and sawdust or for quick decay of brown leaves.

Good garden or woodland soil, although not as high-tech nor as expensive as compost starter, contains native decomposers well able to tackle a compost pile. Sprinkle it among the yard scraps as you are building the pile.

OPTIONAL COMPOST-MAKING EQUIPMENT

Wire composting bin
Stackable composting bin
Wooden composting bin
Vented plastic bins
Worm boxes
Compost tumbler
Compost inoculant
Garden fork
Compost thermometer
Sifting screen

73 **USE PERFORATED PVC PIPES** to aerate compost piles. An ideal compost pile will reach three to four feet high, big enough to get warm from the heat of decay. Why is heat important? High temperatures—when a pile is warm enough to steam on a cool morning, semi-sterilize the developing compost, killing disease spores, hibernating pests, and weed seeds.

But the problem is that in order for decomposers to work efficiently enough to create heat, they need plenty of air—and not just at the surface of the pile. Aeration is traditionally provided by fluffing or turning the pile with a pitchfork, which can be hard work. But with a little advance planning and a perforated pipe, this can be avoided.

Start a compost pile on a bed of branched sticks that will allow air to rise from below. Add a perforated pipe in the center, building layers of old leaves, grass

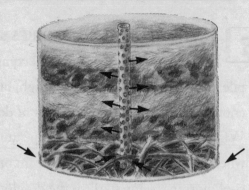

clippings, and other garden leftovers around
it. The air will flow through the pipe into
the pile.

74 **USE ON-SITE COMPOSTING** for
easy soil improvement. Gather up old
leaves, livestock manure, and/or green vegetable scraps and let them lie in or beside the
garden until they rot, then work them into
the soil. Or just heap them on the garden in
the fall and till them into the soil. They will
be decayed by spring. You can also dig a
hole, dump in the yard waste, cover it with
a little soil, and let it rot in privacy.

75 EXPECT TO USE MORE ORGANIC FERTILIZER, by volume, than synthetic chemical fertilizers. That's because organic fertilizers contain fewer nutrients by

COMPOST BLENDS

Organic material decays most quickly if blended with approximately equal parts of the following:

NITROGEN-RICH SOFT AND GREEN MATERIAL

Manure from chickens, cows, horses, rabbits, pigs, guinea pigs, and other herbivores

Fruit and vegetable peels

Grass clippings

Green leaves

Strips of turf

Alfalfa

CARBON-RICH BROWN AND HARD MATERIAL

Wood chips

Ground-up twigs

Sawdust

Pruning scraps

Autumn leaves

Straw

weight, averaging from 1 to about 6 or 7 percent. Contrast this with an inorganic lawn fertilizer that may contain up to 30 percent nitrogen, more than four times as much as organic fertilizer.

More is not always better when it comes to fertilizers. Lower-dose organic fertilizers are unlikely to burn plant roots or cause nutrient overdoses. Many forms release their components slowly, providing a long-term nutrient supply instead of one intense nutrient blast. Organic fertilizers may also provide a spectrum of lesser nutrients, even enzymes and hormones that can benefit growth.

For details on how to use fertilizers properly, read the package labels. The volume of fertilizer required may vary depending on the kind of plant being fertilized and the time of year.

76 **USE FISH EMULSION FERTILIZER** to encourage a burst of growth from new plantings, potted flowers and vegetables, or anything that is growing a little too sluggishly for your taste. High-nitrogen fish emulsion dissolves in water and is easily absorbed and put to immediate use by the plant. For best results, follow the package directions.

77 **ADD TOAD HOUSES** to the garden to attract toads for natural pest control.

Just as fairy-tale toads can be turned into handsome princes with just a kiss, ordinary toads become

plant protectors just by hopping into the garden. They may not be pretty, but toads eat plenty of bugs, so you'll be glad to see them. To encourage toads to come to live in your garden, try the following:

- Put several broken clay pots in the garden for toads to hide under.
- Water when the ground gets dry to keep the environment pleasant for amphibians.
- Avoid spraying toxic chemicals on the garden.
- Watch out for toads when tilling, hoeing, or shoveling.

78 USE ORGANIC REPELLENTS to chase away rodents and deer. Sprays made out of hot peppers, coyote or bobcat urine, rotten eggs, bonemeal, or bloodmeal—even castor oil—can make your garden plants unappetizing to herbivores. Reapply the repellents frequently, and always after rain, to maintain high-protection levels.

79 **GROW FRENCH OR AMERICAN MARIGOLDS** to kill any nematodes in the garden soil. Nematodes—microscopic wormlike pests that can damage tomatoes, potatoes, and other crops—are killed by chemicals that are released by marigold roots and decaying foliage. You can plant marigolds in and around other nematode-susceptible plants. Or just till marigolds into the soil and let them decay before planting potatoes or tomatoes.

CHAPTER 7

PROPAGATION

Starting your own plants from seeds, cuttings, divisions, and layering saves money and expands options. But be prepared to give propagation a certain amount of attention. Young plants, like young children or young puppies, need tender loving care to get them off to a good start.

Many plants grow well from seeds, especially annual flowers, herbs, and vegetables. You can find dozens of new, rare, or old-fashioned varieties in seed catalogues that aren't available in the local nurseries. Seed sowing allows you to grow a few, dozens, or even hundreds of seedlings from a seed packet costing a dollar or two. That's economy!

Certain special plants don't grow from seeds. They need to be cloned (vegetatively propagated). This is done by rooting sections of stems or sprouting chunks of roots. Clump-forming plants can be divided into several pieces, and some stems can be rooted while still attached to the mother plant. The tips included in this chapter will help make the transition from old plant to new as smooth as possible.

80 **KEEP A NOTEBOOK, CALENDAR, OR ADVANCE PLANNER** to remind you when to plant seeds or take cuttings. For example, seeds such as tomatoes and peppers need to be planted six to eight weeks before the last spring frost, but squash and cucumbers need to be planted only three weeks before the last spring frost. It can be hard to remember everything (and squeeze it into your schedule) unless it's written down.

81 **KEEP GOOD PROPAGATION RECORDS** to track how successful each operation has been and how the young plants are proceeding through the seasons. These records will guide you about when to plant, divide, start seeds, or collect seeds for future years. Jot down your observations weekly in a notebook. Or keep an index card on each plant you propagate so it's easy to find the next time. Some gardeners may want to computerize their records. Here are some things to note:

- How long seedlings grew indoors before being transplanted outdoors, and whether that timing allowed enough, too little, or too much time for a great performance outdoors.

- When you planted seedlings outdoors and how well they responded to the weather conditions at that time.

- When the first shoots of perennial flowers and herbs emerged in spring and were ready to divide.

- ❧ When you took stem cuttings from roses, lilacs, geraniums, impatiens, chrysanthemums, dahlias, and other plants. Rooting success often depends on the season in which the cuttings were taken.

- ❧ When seed pods matured and were ready to harvest for next year's crop (see Hint 82).

82 **WATCH THE COLOR OF RIPENING SEED PODS,** which is the clue to when seed is ripe. When dry pods turn from

bright green to
dull green or
brown and suc-
culent fruits turn
bright colors, the
seeds are mature
and ready to
harvest.

107

83 TO KEEP RIPENING SEEDS FROM ESCAPING

when a pod dries and splits
open, slip a net made from an
old nylon stocking over the
seed head. Secure it to the
stem with a twist tie.

84 KEEP DRY SEEDS DRIER by refrigerating

them. This works with both seeds you've
collected from dry pods in the garden and
leftover packaged seeds. Keeping these seeds
in low humidity will encourage a long life-
time. Put collected seeds in dry envelopes.
Keep packaged seeds in their original pack-
ets as long as they are dry. Enclose them in a
sealed plastic bag or glass jar and put them
in the refrigerator, where the air is extra arid.
Avoid putting them in the humidified produce drawers.

85 WHEN PLANTING, LABEL ALL

SEEDS with plant and cultivar name and date sown. Because many seedlings look alike, facing an unlabeled flat would be a nightmare. Labels help you remember such things as which little green sprouts are the zinnias and which are the marigolds.

The cultivar name lets you tell hot peppers from sweet peppers (very important!) and red pansies from blue pansies. Since cultivar names like Hungarian Wax pepper may be too long for short plant labels, come up with code abbreviations (such as "HW pep") and note them in your propagation records for future reference. Write on wooden or plastic tags with permanent ink.

86 **MAKE YOUR OWN LABELS** out of milk cartons or plastic jugs instead of buying them. Simply wash them out, cut them into strips about 1 inch wide and 4 to 6 inches long, and write right on them with permanent ink or wax pencil.

87 **LABEL LIKE THE PROS. WHEN** planting in a flat (see Hint 85), organize plant tags neatly so you can remember which plants they are referring to. If planting the flat with the long side closest to you, run rows of seeds from the front to the back, starting at the left side and ending at the right side. Insert a new label in the planting row each time you start using a different seed. This technique also works for flats of cuttings.

88 **SOW PERENNIAL AND WILD-FLOWER SEEDS OUTDOORS** in raised beds or spacious nursery pots (the

kind you get big flowers in at the nursery)
and let nature get them ready to sprout.
Hardy perennials and wildflowers often have
a special defense called dormancy that keeps
them from sprouting prematurely during a
temporary midwinter thaw (which would be
damaging when the frost returned). They
require a certain amount of cold—or alter-
nating freezing and thawing—to indicate
when winter is truly over and spring has
begun. The easiest way to accommodate the
cold requirement is by putting them outdoors. (For other ways to provide cold treat-
ments, see Hints 90 and 91.)

89 **INSTEAD OF BUYING POTS OR
CELL PACKS,** recycle household containers for starting seedlings. Try some of
the following:

> ❧ Egg crates or milk cartons cut length-
>   wise

❧ Clear plastic bakery containers with
   lids that provide a greenhouselike
   atmosphere
❧ Yogurt cups
❧ Cottage cheese containers
❧ Plastic foam coffee cups

Wash the containers out thoroughly
with soapy water, then sterilize them with a
solution of 1 part bleach to 10 parts water.
Poke holes in the bottom to allow excess
water to drain out.

90 GIVE CERTAIN SUMMER BLOOM-
ING PERENNIALS A BRIEF COLD
CHILL to synchronize their germination.

Provide four weeks of cold, moist conditions (a process called stratification, detailed in Hint 91) to perennials such as asters, goldenrod, sneezeweed, and blazing stars before encouraging them to grow.

91 **TO STRATIFY PERENNIAL SEEDS** that require a cold treatment to germinate, sow them in a community flat of moist seed-starting mix. Label as explained in

SOME PERENNIALS THAT DON'T NEED STRATIFICATION

Lavender	Butterfly weed
Fennel	Purple coneflower
Chives	Orange coneflower
Lemon balm	Rock cress
Oregano	Mountain bluet
Sage	Tickseed 'Early
Catmint	Sunrise'
Germander	Shasta daisy
Valerian	'Snow Lady'

Hint 87. Wrap the entire flat in a plastic bag and close with a twist tie. Set the flat in the refrigerator for the time indicated on the seed packet or in a seed-sowing handbook. When the recommended stratification time is up, move the flat into warmth and bright light so the seeds can sprout and grow.

92 **IF STARTING SEEDS IN A WINDOW,** take extra care to maximize light. Use a south-facing window that will receive sun all day. It should not be blocked by a protruding roof overhang or an evergreen tree or shrub. (Without a south-facing window, it's worth considering building a light garden; see Hint 93.)

Hang foil reflectors behind the flat to keep seedlings from leaning toward the sun. If the seedlings are sitting on a windowsill, make a tent of foil behind them, with the shiny side facing the seedlings. This will

reflect sunlight and illuminate the dark side of the seedlings. They will grow much sturdier and straighter as a result.

93 **START SEEDS INDOORS UNDER LIGHTS** rather than in a window for even, compact growth. Seedlings must have bright light from the moment they peer up out of the soil. In climates with cloudy weather or homes without south-facing windows, sun may not be reliable enough. A light garden is an ideal solution.

Set seedlings snugly under a fluorescent shop light. You could place seedlings on a table or counter and suspend the shop light from the ceiling over them. Or you could set up three or four tiered light stands. You can adapt ordinary shelves by attaching lights to the bottoms of the shelves and growing trays below each light. Put the lights on a timer, set to turn them on for 14 hours a day and off again (one less job for you). You can't beat the results!

94 **MAKE A MINI-GREENHOUSE UNDER LIGHTS** with a clear plastic garment bag. This traps humidity near seedlings, helping to protect them from wilting. To cover nursery flats full of seedlings, bend two wire coat hangers into arches and prop them in the corners of the flat, one at each end. Work the plastic over the top of the hangers, and tuck the loose ends in below the flat.

It's even easier to make a greenhouse cover for individual pots. Slide two sticks (short bamboo stakes work well) into opposite sides of the pot. Then top with the plastic and fold under the pot.

95 **START SEEDS OR CUTTINGS IN AN OLD AQUARIUM OR CLEAR SWEATER BOX** to keep humidity high. Aquariums or sweater boxes are more permanent alternatives to the makeshift options above. They are particularly good for cuttings that may need more overhead and rooting room than seedlings. To reuse these containers, wash them with soapy water, rinse, and sterilize with a solution of 1 part bleach to 10 parts water.

96 **DON'T TRANSPLANT SEEDLINGS** into a larger pot until they have one or two sets of true leaves. This allows seedlings to develop enough roots to be self-supporting even if a few roots are lost in the process. It's also a time when seedling roots are fairly straight and compact, making them easy to separate from nearby plants.

How can you tell when the time is right? It's not as simple as counting the number of leaves on the stem, because the seedling usually has an extra set of leaves called cotyledons or seed leaves. They emerge first and store food that nourishes the sprouting seedlings. When you look closely, you can see that cotyledons are shaped differently from true leaves. Squash seedlings, for instance, have oval squash-seed-shaped cotyledons that are easy to spot. But the true leaves are broad and lobed.

97 **TO AVOID BURNING SEEDLING STEMS** with the salts on your hands or breaking an irreplaceable stem, handle young seedlings by the cotyledon or seed leaf (see Hint 96).

98 **TAKE SOFTWOOD STEM CUTTINGS IN LATE SPRING OR EARLY SUMMER** for fast rooting. New spring shoots are vigorous but soft and suc-culent. They may wilt before they root. But if the shoots are allowed to mature for a month or two, they firm up slightly and are ideal for rooting.

99 **TAKE STEM CUTTINGS IN THE MORNING** when they are fresh and full of water. Once the stem is severed from its root, it will not be able to soak up moisture for several weeks or until new roots develop. If cuttings are started without enough stored moisture, they will simply wilt and die.

100 **USE ROOTING HORMONE ON OLDER OR HARD-TO-ROOT CUTTINGS.** Rooting hormones, available in powdered and liquid forms, contain chemicals (called auxins) that allow cut stems to begin to produce roots. They must be applied as soon as the cutting is taken and before the cutting is put into sterile planting mix. Not all stems need rooting hormone (mints and willows, for instance), but it can make slow starters much more reliable.

101 **AVOID FEEDING SOFTWOOD SHRUB CUTTINGS ANY ADDITIONAL NITROGEN** after rooting. A little

SOME PLANTS SUITABLE FOR SOFTWOOD STEM CUTTINGS

Willows	Chrysanthemums
Maples	Dahlias
Serviceberry	Mints
Clematis	Bee balm
Bugleweed	Catmint
Asters	Lavender
Bellflowers	Bedding geraniums
Blanketflowers	Fuchsias
Hardy geraniums	Tomatoes
Russian sage	Blueberries
Plumbago	

nitrogen, which is available in nutrient-enriched planting mixes, can help the rooting process proceed. But excess nitrogen can encourage fast, tender new growth that is vulnerable to winter damage. Once the cuttings have survived the winter, transplant them into the garden or a larger pot and fertilize them normally.

IO2 **SET A CLEAR GLASS JAR** over cuttings of roses, willows, dogwoods, or other easily rooted stems put directly in the garden. The jar will maintain high humidity around the cutting and help prevent wilting. But be sure to protect the jar from the hot sun so the cuttings don't get cooked.

IO3 **TEST IF A CUTTING HAS ROOTED** by gently tugging on the stem. If it shows resistance, roots have formed. After first rooting, allow the roots to develop for several more weeks, if possible, before transplanting.

IO4 **TAKE ROOT CUTTINGS** when stem cuttings are not possible. Some perennials, like Oriental poppies and horseradish, have clusters of foliage close to the ground without any stems at all. You can dig up a root and cut it into pieces that may sprout into new plants. With horseradish, you can cut off a side root in the fall and replant it for a new start in the spring. But root cuttings of most other perennials need more help than horseradish. Here's how to do it:

- Dig the root in early spring before shoots begin to emerge.

- Cut the roots into pieces an inch or two long.

- Lay them horizontally in a flat of well-drained propagating mix such as perlite or coarse sand. Cover lightly.

- Keep slightly moist but not wet (to prevent root rot) and watch for new sprouts to emerge.
- When the new plants are growing strongly, transplant them into individual containers or put them out in the garden.

105 **"HARDEN OFF" SEEDLINGS AND CUTTINGS** before they go out into the garden. When growing in the protection of a windowsill, light garden, or greenhouse, young plants are tender and can be easily damaged by strong winds or sun. Toughen them up (a process called hardening off) to make the transition from indoors to outdoors successful.

- Days 1 and 2: Put well-watered young plants outdoors in a shady location for several hours. Bring them back indoors when the time is up.

- Days 3 and 4: Increase the length of time seedlings stay outdoors in the shade.
- Days 5 to 7: When well adjusted to shade, gradually move sun-loving plants into brighter light, starting with an hour of sun the first day.
- Days 8 and beyond: When seedlings can stay out all day without burning or wilting, they are ready for transplanting.

106 **EASILY DIVIDE DAYLILIES, HOSTAS, ASTILBES,** or other clump-forming perennials with a sharp shovel. Just slice off an edge of the clump in spring or late summer. Uproot it and replant elsewhere. Keep the new division watered for at least several weeks or until it has regenerated lost roots.

107 **DIVIDE A LARGE PERENNIAL CLUMP** into small divisions to get many little plants fast. This is a quick and easy way to make enough plants for the big drifts, clumps, or ground covers that are so popular in landscaping today.

A mature bee balm clump might contain 50 rooted sprouts, each of which can be separated off and grown into a new plant. Other easily divided perennials include asters, daylilies, yarrow, phlox, lady's mantle, salvia, coreopsis, hardy geraniums, irises, mint, thyme, oregano, and winter savory. Here's how to make smaller divisions:

🌢 In spring or late summer, dig up the entire perennial plant clump and wash soil off the roots with a hose.

- ❧ If dividing in late summer, cut back the foliage by half or more.

- ❧ Use your hands to break rooted sprouts into individual pieces. If roots are too hard to work apart by hand, slice them free with a knife or pruning shears. Each section should contain at least one leafy sprout and one healthy root.

- ❧ Replant very small divisions into pots of peat-based planting mix and tend them carefully until they get a little bigger. Larger divisions can go right back into the garden if kept moist until they become reestablished.

108 **ROOT THE PLANTLETS ON SPIDER PLANTS** and strawberry begonias, which grow from the parent plant on arching stems. These pretty plantlets have leaves but no roots, a condition that's easy to correct. Put a pot of peat-based potting mix beside the parent plant and set the plantlet in it. Firm the mix around the lower part of the plantlet and keep it moist. Once the plantlet roots, snip the stem and enjoy.

109 USE LAYERING TO PROPAGATE HARD-TO-ROOT SHRUBS like azaleas. Layering also works well with shrubs that have low-growing or creeping branches, like creeping rosemary. Layered stems develop roots while still connected to the mother plant, which helps nourish the rooting process.

- In spring, select a low, flexible branch that will bend down to the ground easily.
- Prepare well-drained but moisture-retentive soil where the stem will touch the ground.
- Nick the bark off the side of the stem that will touch the ground and remove the leaves near the nick. Dust the cut

with rooting hormone (see Hint 100).

- Cover the barren and nicked stem with soil. Top it with a rock or pin it in place with a stake or metal pin.

- The branch tip will become the new plant. If it is an upright grower, stake the tip upright to give it a good shape.

- Keep the rooting area moist for several months, until roots develop and become large enough to the support the new plant.

- Cut the new plant free from the parent branch and transplant it to a pot or new site in the garden.

CHAPTER 8

PESTS AND DISEASES

Growing healthy plants is the first step toward a great garden. In order to achieve this, it's important to prevent diseases and pests through careful plant selection, planting, and care. It also helps to use some of the environmentally safe new products and techniques described in this chapter.

Among the most important considerations when preventing diseases is soil drainage (see Hint 6); soggy roots lead to rot in almost every instance (though there are some plants that need the extra water). Sunlight is also essential. It must keep the plant well nourished (by photosynthesizing) so it can stay robust enough to resist diseases that attack weak plants.

Plants with enough space to reach maturity without overcrowding are likely to be healthy. They suffer less competition with their neighbors for sun, water, and nutrients, and they enjoy plenty of fresh air. In an over-crowded garden, airflow stagnates, just as it does in an overcrowded room. Without free air circulation, foliage dampened by dew, rain, or sprinkling will stay wet longer and be more susceptible to fungus and other diseases.

110 **CHOOSE DISEASE-RESISTANT CULTIVARS** whenever possible. They are bred to resist infection—an ideal way to avoid diseases. Growing disease-resistant vegetables prevents chemical tainting of your food. Disease-resistant varieties of popular flowers such as roses save you time, trouble, and expense.

There are varying levels of protection available:

- Some cultivars have multiple disease resistances for maximum protection.

SOME DISEASE–RESISTANT CULTIVARS

ROSES: 'The Fairy,' 'Red Fairy,' rugosa roses, 'Carefree Delight,' David Austin English Roses, Town and Country Roses, Meidiland roses

ZINNIAS: 'Star Gold,' 'Star Orange,' 'Star White,' 'Crystal White,' 'Cherry Pinwheel,' 'Salmon Pinwheel,' 'Rose Pinwheel,' 'Orange Pinwheel'

CUCUMBERS: 'Park's All-Season Burpless Hybrid,' 'Fancipack,' 'Homemade Pickles,' 'Tasty King,' 'Sweet Success,' 'Salad Bush'

PEAS: 'Super Sugar Snap,' 'Sugar Pop,' 'Maestro,' 'Green Arrow'

BEANS: 'Florence,' 'Buttercrisp,' 'Jade'

TOMATOES: 'Celebrity,' 'Better Boy,' 'LaRossa,' 'Enchantment,' 'Sunmaster,' 'Mountain Delight,' 'Big Beef,' 'Beefmaster,' 'Sweet Million,' 'Viva Italia,' 'Roma'

APPLES: 'Liberty,' 'Jonafree,' 'MacFree,' 'Freedom'

STRAWBERRIES: 'Surecrop,' 'Cavendish,' 'Redchief,' 'Allstar,' 'Guardian,' 'Scott,' 'Lateglow,' 'Delite'

The 'Big Beef' tomato, for instance, resists various types of wilts: tobacco mosaic virus, nematodes, and gray leaf spot. Little is left that can harm it.

🌿 Some cultivars resist only one disease. But if that disease is a problem in your area, then these plants will be worth their weight in gold.

🌿 Other plants are disease tolerant, meaning they may still get the disease but should grow well despite it.

To find out more about disease-resistant cultivars for your area, ask your local Cooperative Extension Service or a knowledgeable professional grower. Or get your name on the mailing list for nursery and seed catalogues that describe disease-resistant cultivars.

 III **INTERPLANT HERBS AND FLOWERS WITH VEGETABLES** to help reduce pest problems. This gives the vegetable garden a colorful patchwork look and helps confuse problem pests. The varied aromas of interplantings make it hard for pests to find their favorite food by scent. This works particularly well if you interplant with powerfully fragrant herbs and flowers such as mints, basils, lemon geraniums, garlic, or onions.

112 ATTRACT BENEFICIAL INSECTS.

Sprinkling flowering plants amid the garden helps draw ladybugs, spiders, lacewings, and tiny parasitic wasps who prey on plant-eating pests. The flowers provide shelter plus nectar and pollen, an alternative food source.

Once beneficial insects are at home in your garden, keep them there. Remember, they can be killed as quickly as plant pests by broad-spectrum pesticides, which kill indiscriminately. It's best to avoid pesticides or use targeted pesticides such as Bt (a bacterial disease of caterpillars that won't harm other insects) to protect beneficial insects.

113 **USE FLOATING ROW COVERS** to keep pests off vegetables. This simple idea works so well it's a wonder nobody thought of it years ago. Floating row covers are lightweight fabrics that you can drape over plants. They allow sun, rain, and fresh air to penetrate, but if secured to the ground with rocks, bricks, or long metal staples, they will keep flying insects out. Here are some great ways to use floating row covers:

🌢 Eliminate maggots (fly larvae) that will tunnel into the roots of radishes, turnips, carrots, onions, and other vegetables. Row covers keep egg-laying female flies away from the vegetables. If there are no eggs, there are no maggots.

- Keep potato beetles from eating the foliage off potato leaves and vines. Pin the row cover edges down tightly so the beetles can't crawl under.
- Protect cucumbers, squash, and pumpkins from cucumber beetles, which carry a wilt disease capable of killing entire vines. Since flowers of these vines need insect pollination for fruit set, the covers must be lifted for several hours at least every other day for honeybees to do their work.

114 **USE BARRIERS OF COPPER STRIPS OR DIATOMACEOUS EARTH** to keep slugs away from plants. Slugs are voracious plant eaters. They eat almost anything, ganging up on tender succulent plants and eating them down to the ground. They thrive where soils are damp, spending sunny days under rocks, logs, or mulch and coming out to eat

when it's rainy or cool and dark. Any slug
control measures you use will work better
if you clear out excess mulch and any dark,
dank hiding places where slugs might breed.

🌿 Diatomaceous earth is a gritty substance that pierces
the skin of soft-
bodied slugs.
Sprinkle it
on the
soil, encir-
cling plants
plagued by slugs.
Use horticultural-grade diatomaceous
earth, not the kind sold in swimming
pool stores.

🌿 Copper strips, set around the edge of
the garden, prevent slug trespass by
creating an unpleasant reaction when
touched with the mucus on the crawling
slugs. Set copper strips an inch deep

and several inches high so that slugs can't get over or under the copper strips.

115 **KILL EXISTING SLUGS** by trapping them in deep saucers of beer. Slugs love beer, and that can be their downfall. Bury an empty plastic margarine tub in the garden soil. The top rim should be level with the soil surface. Fill the tub with beer (any kind will do) and leave it overnight. The slugs will crawl in and drown. Empty the tub every day or two and refill with beer until the tub comes through the night empty.

116 **SPRAY APHIDS OFF PLANTS** with a strong stream of water. Aphids, small sap-sucking insects with soft, pear-shaped bodies, cling to succulent young stems and buds. They reproduce quickly, sometimes covering stems that curl and distort in protest. Because aphids can multiply into swarms almost overnight, it's important to eliminate any that you find.

Before hauling out any pesticides, try a strong blast of water from the hose. Aphids are easily dislodged from plants. This method works best on mature or woody plants that won't be damaged by the force of the water blast. Repeat every couple of days or any time you see new aphids arriving.

117 **SPRAY PLANTS SUSCEPTIBLE TO FOLIAGE FUNGUS** with wilt-proofing solution before disease strikes. This product is a pine oil modified to spread into a film coating that protects evergreen foliage from drying out during winter. An unexpected side effect of the film is that it keeps fungus spores from penetrating into susceptible leaves. Mix according to label directions and try it on phlox, bee balm, cucumbers, watermelons, tomatoes, and apples. Do not, however, spray plants with hairy leaves.

118 **EXPERIMENT WITH BAKING SODA SPRAYS** to prevent fungus diseases. Mix two teaspoons baking soda in 2 quarts of water with $1/2$ teaspoon corn oil. Shake well, put in a sprayer, and go to work. Spray susceptible plants often and always after rain to help keep diseases such as powdery mildew from getting started.

119 **THIN STEMS ON DISEASE-PRONE PLANTS** to improve air circulation. Mildew-susceptible phlox and bee balm, for instance, can grow into clumps so thick that they block air flow. This encourages fungus attack, but it is easily corrected. When new growth is coming up in the spring, cut out every third stem, targeting those that are weak or in areas of the thickest growth.

120 **USE BAGS OF SOAP OR HUMAN HAIR** to repel deer. Sometimes called jack rabbits on hooves, deer seem to enjoy

---

SOME PLANTS PREFERRED BY DEER

Fraser and balsam firs	Evergreen azaleas
Norway maple	Hybrid tea rose
Redbud	European mountain ash
Clematis	Yews
Winged euonymus	Arborvitaes
Wintercreeper	Asters
English ivy	Hostas
Apples	Phlox
Cherries	Lilies
Plums	Tulips
Rhododendrons	

dining on cultivated plants and are worst in the winter, gobbling evergreens when their native food supply dwindles. But they are also a problem in spring and summer when they like to munch tender flowers and new growth. In fall, males rub their antlers on wood and can damage small trees and shrubs. However, they don't enjoy strong-smelling soaps and human hair.

Powerfully scented soap can be stuffed in a mesh bag and dangled from branches about 3 feet high. You also can set soap bars directly on the ground. Replenish the soap supply frequently so it won't dissolve away or lose its smell.

You can also fill mesh bags with human hair. Hang them outside (like a furry scarecrow) so deer wonder if you are hiding in the garden. Refill bags as soon as you pull another handful from your hairbrush.

CHAPTER 9

GARDEN DESIGN

Growing plants beautifully is a wonderful thing, but arranging them in a handsome landscape is even better. A good landscape design plays many roles. It blends the house into the yard, making the entire property look good and increasing property values. Through the design of the landscape, you can create outdoor privacy with hedges, fences, vine-covered trellises, or informal clusters of plants that act like walls of an outdoor room. You can seclude certain areas of the yard or buffer the entire property perimeter.

Landscape designs might include work areas, places for composting or vegetable gardening, even areas for storing trash cans and other less-than-decorative necessities. You can designate places for entertaining—

decks, patios, barbecue pits, or perhaps a
white garden for guests to enjoy on a moon-
lit night. You can even have areas groomed
especially for the dog or the children's play
equipment.

Once you make a list of what you want
in your yard, you can begin to find the room
for it all and start getting all the elements in
place.

121 **DRAW A MAP OF YOUR PROPERTY**
and choose where the new beds and
plantings will go before you start buying and
planting. The map needs to be to scale, an
exact replica of your property in miniature.
Many designers use a scale in which 1/4-inch
on the plan equals one foot in your yard. This
scale usually provides enough room to show
considerable detail but is likely to require the
use of oversized paper to fit everything on
one sheet.

❧ GARDEN DESIGN ❧

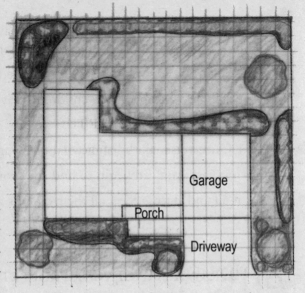

Measure the yard using a measuring
tape (50-foot lengths work well) and sketch
the perimeter on graph paper. Draw in existing trees, shrubs, fences, and other features
you intend to keep. Make some copies so
you can experiment with designs. Then
pencil in possible bed outlines and imagine
how they will look. Once you've decided on
the location of the beds, pencil in the plants
you want to add (at the proper spacing) and

146

get an accurate count of how many plants you'll need before you start shelling out any money.

122 **PLAN THE SHAPE OF THE LAWN,** which is usually the biggest feature in a yard. The lawn's shape is more important than the shape of the beds. If it's designed with straight or gradually curving lines, the lawn can make a pretty picture and remain easy to mow. Avoid sharp turns, wiggly edges, and jagged corners that are irritating to the eye and extra work to mow.

123 **TAKE PHOTOS AND PHOTOCOPY THEM.** You can shoot the entire front yard or backyard, the plantings around the house's foundation, or individual gardens. Enlarge them on a color copier, if one is available. Then you can sketch in prospective new plants and get an idea of how they will

look. A great
time to do this
is in winter.
Although the
yard may be
dormant, you
won't forget
how it looks.

124 **BORROW IDEAS FROM NEIGH-BORS' GARDENS.** There is no better way to learn what grows well in your area. You also can get great design ideas from other people. Remember, mimicry is the greatest form of flattery.

125 **VISIT PUBLIC GARDENS** and nurseries with display beds for inspiration. These professionally designed gardens may have the newest plants and creative ideas for combining them. Look for gardens about the same size as your yard so you can apply what you learn directly.

126 **MATCH THE FLOWERING PLANT TO THE SITE.** Most flowers are high-performance plants, especially sensitive to inadequacies in light, moisture, soil, or other elements. Give them exactly what they need to thrive (see Hint 1).

127 **SELECT FLOWERING PLANTS WITH A RANGE OF BLOOM TIMES** to keep the garden interesting through the seasons. Many perennials, shrubs, and trees will flower for a maximum of three weeks per year. (Some exceptions are in the list on this page.) On paper, list those that bloom in early and late spring, early and late summer, early and late fall. Then when you plant your garden, you can develop a sequence so one kind of flower will fade as another begins to open.

Annual flowers are great for filling the gaps. Pansies, sweet alyssum, and calendula thrive in cool spring and fall weather. Petunias, marigolds, zinnias, geraniums, and other annuals will fill the frost-free summer months with color. And tender bulbs such as dahlias and cannas can also provide bright color through much of the warm summer season.

PERENNIALS WITH EXCEPTIONALLY LONG BLOOM

Orange coneflowers	Blanketflower
Purple coneflowers	'Stella de Oro' daylily
Coreopsis	Russian sage
Rose mallow hibiscus	Stoke's aster
Lenten rose	Pincushion flower
Violet sage	'Sunny Border Blue' veronica
Sedum x 'Autumn Joy'	
Asters	Spiderwort
'Luxuriant' bleeding heart	

128 **CHOOSE FLOWERING PLANTS**
with good foliage as well as flowers. The
foliage will still be on display long after the
flowers are gone. For starters, find plants
with foliage that stays healthy, lush, and
green and won't become off-colored, ragged,
or diseased after flowering. Then you can
expand to add plants with golden, silver,
bronze, blue, or multicolored leaves that fit
the garden color scheme.

129 **PLANT TREES AND SHRUBS FIRST,**
then add flower gardens. Woody plants
are the bones of the garden, the bold foundation that will be there summer and winter
to enclose your yard or blend your house
into the property. They are also the most
expensive and permanent features and, as
such, need to be given special priority. Plan
well, find top-quality trees and shrubs, and
plant them properly where they can thrive.

130 MAKE ISLAND BEDS HALF AS WIDE as the distance from where you view them.

Island beds, often oval or kidney-shaped, are situated in areas of lawn where they can be viewed from all sides. They may be near a corner of your yard or by your driveway or entrance walk.

No matter where you put it, an island bed needs to be wide enough to look substantial from your house, patio, or kitchen window—wherever you usually are when

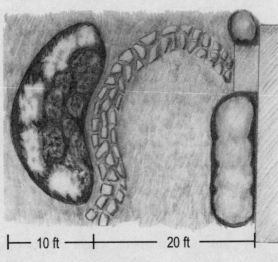

├─ 10 ft ─┤   20 ft ─────┤

you see it. A tiny garden located far from the
house is more comical than beautiful. So, for
example, if an island bed is 20 feet away,
make it 10 feet across. In very large yards,
keep island beds closer to the house if you
don't have time to tend a large island bed.

131 **MAKE BORDERS UP TO HALF AS
WIDE** as the total space in a small- or
medium-sized yard. For example, a 40-foot-
wide yard could have one border 20 feet

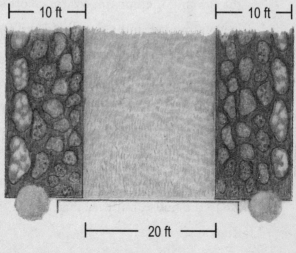

├— 10 ft —┤   ├— 10 ft —┤

├— 20 ft —┤

wide or two borders 10 feet wide. Borders—
traditional gardens usually set at the edge of
a yard, fence, or hedge—also need enough
size to be in scale and make an impact in the
yard. Wider borders can accommodate taller
plants, including trees, shrubs, and large
clumps of perennials and ornamental grasses,
taking on a rich diversity.

132 **USE WARM COLORS AND COOL
COLORS** to give the garden just the
right amount of emphasis. Warm colors such
as yellow, orange, and red are bold and appear visually to be closer to you than they
are. This makes them ideal for a garden
located farther away from your house. Cool
colors such as blue and purple recede from
the eye and look farther away than they
really are. They make pleasant, quiet gardens
close to the house, but they may be lost
farther away.

You can blend cool and warm colors to give a feeling of movement and depth in the garden. Color blends also provide vivid contrast, which some people find exhilarating.

133 **CONSIDER VARYING LEAF SIZES** for more design interest. Large leaves like those on hostas or oak leaf hydrangeas advance and stand out (similar to warm-colored flowers). They are striking in prominent locations, but if overused they will lose their impact.

Small or finely textured leaves, as on thread leaf coreopsis or carrot tops, recede from the eye and look farther away. They can best be appreciated up close. Or if you are trying to make a garden look deeper, these varieties might be used toward the rear as a floral optical illusion. But when used exclusively, fine textured leaves may look busy and weedy.

134 ADD IN THE IMPACT OF FLOWER SIZE to get another variable for an interesting design. Large flowers are bold and prominent. Smaller flowers and fine flower clusters recede. Blending airy small flower sprays with large, bold flowers combines the best of both textures. Planting larger flowers toward the front of a garden and smaller flowers toward the rear increases visual depth.

135 USE A COLLECTION OF POTS to end cut-throughs and shortcuts. Gaps in the shrubbery or fencing around your yard are an invitation for neighborhood kids to slip through. Even adults will be tempted to shortcut across the lawn instead of following a longer path up the walk. Reroute traffic by blocking openings and detours with large pots of plants, flowers, herbs, or even your indoor floor plants brought outside in the

summer.
Cluster
them to-
gether in a
barrier
that's not

easily skirted. As a bonus, you'll have a dynamic plant grouping with maximum impact
in the landscape.

136 USE OLD CONCRETE from a poured
sidewalk as stepping stones in a bed or
border. This faux stone is either given away
or sold inexpensively by communities con-
ducting sidewalk renovation. Other people
may have the same idea, so call well before
you need the concrete and get your name on
a waiting list if necessary.

137 CREATE A SHADE GARDEN WITH-
OUT TREES by planting under a vine-

covered arbor. Shade gardens can feature serene blends of ferns, hostas, and woodland wildflowers, plus a few dazzling bloomers such as azaleas and rhododendrons. Although these plants usually grow amid trees and shrubs, they can thrive in shadows cast by other structures—walls, fences, houses, or a vine-covered arbor.

The advantage of an arbor shade garden is that fewer roots are competing for moisture and nutrients. And unlike a planting close to a wall or building, the arbor shade garden has plenty of fresh air circulation. In addition, an arbor looks great when clad in flowers and handsome foliage.

VINES FOR AN ARBOR

Clematis | Kolomikta vine
Trumpet creeper | Silver-lace vine
Honeysuckle | Wisteria
Climbing roses | Jasmine (warm
Kiwi vines | climate only)

138 COVER ROCKS AND BRICKS WITH
MOSS using a buttermilk-moss milkshake. A soft green moss veneer adds an air
of antiquity, permanence, and beauty to
walls, walks, or woodland rock gardens. You
can wait a few years for moss to naturally
creep into moist and shady places, or you
can encourage a quicker appearance. Gather
local cushion-forming mosses, the kinds that
thrive in your climate, and find a garden
location similar to where they naturally
grow. Mix the moss with buttermilk in a
blender and pour the concoction onto the
appropriate rocks or bricks in your garden.

Let it dry thoroughly. Keep the area moist, but not so wet that the milkshake washes off the bricks or stones. New moss will soon make an appearance.

139 **REDUCE THE VOLUME OF STRONG WINDS** by planting a layered assortment of plants as a windbreak. Wind can knock down and dry out plants, generally making it harder to get the garden to grow well. Layered plants—taller trees with shade-tolerant shrubs planted under them—create an irregular barrier that gently stops wind. Solid fences, in contrast, allow wind to slip up and over and swirl back in on the other side.

140 **PLANT BAMBOO FOR A QUICK SCREEN.** Bamboo has handsome foliage and grows in upright thickets that can provide quick and easy privacy. But most types of bamboo are vigorous spreaders. To keep them from overwhelming a garden, plant them in large, submerged tubs or pots that keep the roots contained.

141 **DON'T FORGET TO PLACE A BENCH** in the garden. You can sit and admire your handiwork, which always looks best up close. Your bench, even a rugged one, can double as garden sculpture.

TYPES OF
GARDENS

A landscape is the sum of its many parts: lawn; flower and vegetable gardens; vines and ground covers; shrub borders and hedges; and shade or ornamental trees. Each is an important element in its own right, and each contributes to the collective beauty and usefulness of the landscape.

A lush, green lawn enhances the beauty of all else around it, and though it may be overlooked for other, more "showy" forms of vegetation, the lawn is the basic element in your landscape, bringing everything else together.

Vegetable, fruit, and herb gardens yield flavorful harvests. They can be simple working gardens or handsomely constructed decorative elements. Flower gardens provide color, beauty, bouquets for the house, and food for birds and butterflies. Shrubs can be backdrops for flower or vegetable gardens, or they can serve as ornaments in their own right.

Knowing the potential of each landscape element allows you to utilize them for the best effect, making the most out of your garden.

CHAPTER 10

LAWNS

The emerald green lawn that spreads across most people's yards serves many purposes: It gives us places to play, filters air pollution, cools the air, and softens harsh light. But healthy, beautiful lawns don't just happen; they require work—more than just about any other part of the yard.

We have become accustomed to fertilizing, spraying, and mowing. This kind of pampering can result in a lush and pristine lawn, but it may also be more time-consuming than is necessary.

If you're planting a new lawn and want it to be low-maintenance, choose the right kind of grass for the site, plant at the ideal time, and use organic and slow-releasing fertilizers. Or, if you're dealing with an existing lawn,

follow our easy hints to learn how to minimize maintenance.

142 **USE A MIXTURE OF TURF GRASSES**
for a disease-resistant lawn. Diseases
that attack one type of grass may not affect
the others, so you are reducing risks.

Grass blends also increase versatility. Fine
fescues mixed with bluegrass, for instance, are
less likely to turn brown in summer heat. Read
the labels on lawn grass seed packages closely
to identify which grass mixtures are used and
how they might affect performance.

143 **PLANT CREEPING RED FESCUE** in a
lightly shaded lawn where bluegrass is
likely to fail. For best results, provide well-
drained, slightly acidic soil.

144 **CONSIDER THE MERITS OF SOD,
SEED, AND PLUGS** before choosing

which to use to start a new lawn:

🌿 Sod: Sheets of prestarted turf can be
purchased ready to be laid out on pre-

GRASSES FOR
DIFFERENT PURPOSES

COOL CLIMATES: SUN
Kentucky bluegrass

COOL CLIMATES: SUN OR LIGHT SHADE
Chewings fescue
Creeping red fescue

MODERATE CLIMATES: SUN OR LIGHT SHADE
Hard fescue
Tall fescue

WARM CLIMATES: SUN
Bermuda grass
Zoysia grass

WARM CLIMATES: SUN OR LIGHT SHADE
St. Augustine grass

BALL FIELDS
Perennial ryegrass

GOLF COURSES
Creeping bent grass

---

pared soil, where they will take root and grow. Sod is expensive, but it provides an "instant lawn," and many people like that. It's great on a slope where grass seed can be washed away with the first heavy rain. But sod has a few potential problems in addition to its high cost. It may fail to thrive on difficult soils, and your selection can be limited to a few varieties and blends.

🌢 Seed: Grass seed is inexpensive and available in a wide variety of custom mixes; there's something for every kind of lawn. It is best planted in warm, mild weather and must be kept constantly moist to germinate. The grass needs to become well established before summer heat or winter cold push it to the limits.

🌢 Plugs: These are small clumps of sod that can be planted like a ground cover

in prepared soil. If
kept moist and
fertilized, the
plugs will
spread
to form
a solid sheet of turf. Plugs are an important way of starting warm-climate lawns
and a way to economize in cooler climates.

145 **USE SEED RATHER THAN SOD** to
establish grass on poor soils. Sod roots
may never grow into stiff clay soils, which
puts a damper on their future if drought
strikes. Spend a little extra time and money
to improve poor soil with compost and peat
moss. Then plant seed of suitable grasses
and tend the lawn well (feeding, watering,
raking, and weeding, as necessary) until it is
growing strongly.

146 **USE EDGINGS** to keep grass out of garden beds. A physical barrier can prevent sprigs of grass from spreading to unwanted areas where they can make bed edges look ragged or spring up amid other plants.

Edgings made of 5- to 6-inch-wide strips of fiberglass, metal, or plastic—even stones or brick—can line the perimeter of a garden bed. Let the upper edge emerge a little above the soil (but well below the level of the mower) and the lower edge sink securely into the ground. More ex-pensive edgings should last longer than cheap plastics, which can shift out of place during winter.

147 **TOP-DRESS THE LAWN** with compost or rotted manure to keep it healthy. Unlike super-concentrated fertilizers that stimulate rapid growth, these natural fertilizers provide light doses of nutrients and improve soil conditions. Make sure the compost or manure is finely screened so it will settle down to the soil without packing on top of the turf.

148 **FERTILIZE LAWNS WITH SLOW-RELEASE NITROGEN FERTILIZER.** Slow-release products gradually emit moderate amounts of nitrogen over a period of weeks or months, so you won't need to fertilize as often. The nitrogen levels in slow-release products are high enough to keep your yard green and healthy, but not so high that the lawn is stimulated to grow rampantly and require continual mowing. Read fertilizer bag labels carefully to determine which brands contain slow-release nitrogen.

149 **FILL IN LOW SPOTS** in uneven lawns by spreading sand evenly over the lawn area with a metal rake. You can sprinkle grass seed on the sand or wait for the surrounding grasses to send out new tillers and colonize the fill.

150 **LEAVE GRASS BLADES LONGER** for more drought resistance and better root growth. Longer blades shade the soil and roots, keeping them cooler and moister, and the grass roots may grow deeper. In contrast, close-cropped lawns can dry out quickly in summer heat. The stubby leaves expose grass-free openings where crabgrass and other weeds can grow.

151 **KEEP YOUR LAWN MOWER BLADES SHARP.** Like a sharp razor on a day-old beard, your mower will slice through grass blades, giving a clean, level cut. Dull blades tear grasses, which can increase their susceptibility to diseases.

152 **DETHATCH YOUR LAWN** once a year or as needed to keep it healthy. Thatch is a layer of dead grass stalks that can build up at the soil surface, cutting off air, water, and fertilizer when it becomes thick and matted. Thatch can also harbor pests.

A vigorous raking can help break up small amounts of thatch. For big problems, you can rent dethatching machines. Use them in mild weather and plan to reseed if necessary to refill gaps left behind. Once thatch is gone, the clippings can rot to enrich the soil.

153 **DON'T MOW THE LAWN DURING DROUGHT.** Without rainfall, the grass is unlikely to grow much, if any.

154 **WATER SPARINGLY DURING DROUGHT.** Providing about a half inch of water every two weeks can keep grass alive without encouraging growth.

155 **AERATE COMPACTED LAWNS** to keep them healthy. With a lot of foot or wheel traffic, soil can become hard-packed, creating a poor environment for grass roots. To help air reach the roots (and also to cut out old thatch), run over the lawn with a core cultivator.

This is a machine that pulls up small cylinders of soil, creating breathing spaces. Do-it-yourselfers can buy or rent a core cultivator (see the illustration at right). As an alternative, have a landscaper or lawn-care company core your yard.

156 **TRY A FRAGRANT HERBAL LAWN** for a change of pace. Herbal lawns release delightful fragrances when you walk on them or mow them. But few herbs will tolerate as much traffic as grass, so it's best to keep them out of the mainstream. You can blend low-growing creeping herbs into grass or plant a smaller area entirely in herbs.

HERBS FOR A FRAGRANT LAWN

Creeping thyme	Clover
Roman chamomile	Yarrow
Mint	Pennyroyal

157 **TURN A RAGGED LAWN INTO A** meadow by killing the grass and planting perennial wildflowers and grasses (see Hint 66). This works best in the privacy of your backyard or in country settings.

158 **CONSIDER MOWING WITH A HAND-POWERED REEL MOWER.** On a well-tended lawn, reel mowers provide an especially polished cut. They are also quiet and energy efficient.

VEGETABLES

Whether you like to cook or just to eat, a vegetable garden can be the perfect addition to your yard. Situate it in a sunny place, raise the beds so you can start growing food early in spring, then keep planting all summer long so something fresh is always ready to harvest.

Spring is a wonderful time for succulent, tender lettuces, spinach, and asparagus. In summer, you can pick juicy tomatoes and fruity ripe peppers. And in fall, salad gardening time returns with great radishes, carrots, and more lettuce.

But fresh and flavorful produce is just the beginning. Growing your own vegetables organically ensures healthful produce and saves you the high prices of organically grown produce at the grocery store.

> ## *VEGETABLES: FLAVORFUL AND ATTRACTIVE*
>
> Experiment with vegetables that are extra pretty or extra flavorful, such as the following:
>
> • Ruby- and pink-leaved lettuces
> • Green, yellow, and purple snap beans; the purple ones turn green when cooked
> • Crimson, white, gold, and red-striped beets
> • Violet, neon pink, soft pink, and white eggplants
> • Peppers ranging from sweet to mild spicy to super hot—something for everyone
> • Red, orange, yellow, pink, or cream tomatoes; for exceptional flavor, try 'Brandywine' and 'Sweet 100' cherry tomatoes

Add walks and arbors and interplant with beautiful flowers and herbs to make the vegetable garden both pretty and productive.

159 **KEEP THE GARDEN NEAR YOUR KITCHEN.** It will be easy to run out and pick a few things you need, and you can spy on the garden from your window. Picking tomatoes after you see them blush crimson is a perfect way to get them at their best.

160 **SOAK SEEDS** to get a jump on the season. Before germinating, seeds need to drink up moisture, just as if drenched by spring rains. Once they become plump and swollen, the little embryo inside will begin to grow.

Seeds such as broccoli, cabbage, and arugula use moisture efficiently and germinate promptly without presoaking. But slower-starting parsley and parsnip seeds benefit from presoaking. Dunk them in room-temperature water for several hours or even overnight, but don't forget them and leave them in too long. Drain and plant the seeds immediately.

161 **PRODUCE LATE FALL, WINTER, AND EARLY SPRING LETTUCE** by growing extra-hardy varieties such as 'Artic

King' or 'North Pole,' and creating sheltered planting places for them:

- ✿ Raised beds covered with heavy-duty floating row covers can provide protection from frosts and light freezes in early to mid-spring and mid- to late fall, or even winter in mild climates.

- ✿ Cold frames, heated by the sun, make it possible to grow lettuce early in spring and later in  fall or winter. Cold frames are translucent rectangular boxes, about 2 feet wide, 4 feet long, and 18 inches high. The top is hinged to open so you can tend plants inside or cool the cold frame on mild, sunny days. Plant seeds or seedlings of lettuce in the frame and shut the lid to hold in the heat.

❧ A hot bed, which is a souped-up cold frame, is a great place for winter lettuce. Lay a heating cable under the cold frame. Cover with wire mesh to prevent damage to the cable, and top with a layer of sand mixed with compost.

162 **USE WATER-FILLED TEPEES** around tender vegetables for protection from the cold. You can buy inexpensive plastic sheets of connected tubes that, when filled with water, form self-supporting walls around seedlings. The clear walls allow sun to penetrate to the plant inside while the solar-heated water stays warm into the night.

163 **START WITH LARGE SEEDLINGS** for quick results in cold climates. This strategy works well for tender vegetables like beefsteak tomatoes and chili peppers that take a long time to ripen but must squeeze in their performance before the last curtain—frost—does them in for the season.

Look for seedlings grown in large pots (indicating a strong root system) with healthy green leaves and a sturdy constitution. Avoid neglected, overgrown seedlings.

Note that not every seedling transplants well when older. Cucumbers, squash, zucchini, pumpkins, and gourds are best started from young seedlings planted carefully to minimize root disturbance.

164 **MULCH ASPARAGUS EVERY SPRING** with several inches of compost or decayed livestock manure. Asparagus, a greedy feeder, will use all the nutrients it can get its roots on and grow that much better for it. By mulching in the spring, you can fertilize, help keep the soil moist, and reduce weed seed germination all in one effort. The shoots that arise through the mulch will grow especially plump and succulent.

165 **MAKE FANCY WHITE ASPARAGUS SPEARS** with a simple blanching basket. This European connoisseur item is easy to do at home. When the spears first emerge in spring, cover them with a bucket, basket, or mound of soil that will exclude all light. Harvest when the spears reach 8 to 10 inches tall and before the ferny leaves begin to emerge.

166 **TEAR THE TOPS AND BOTTOMS OFF PEAT POTS** when setting out vegetables. Peat pots, which are supposed to decay when submerged in the soil, don't always break down the first year they are planted. This leaves plant roots captive inside. To complicate matters further, if the peat rim emerges above the soil surface, it can dry out and steal moisture from the surrounding soil and nearby roots. Peat pot problems are easily solved by tearing off the top and bottom of the pot before planting. This helps eliminate the danger of drying out and gives roots a way to escape if the peat pot persists.

167 **PLANT LEGGY VEGETABLE SEEDLINGS DEEPER** to provide a stronger start outdoors. Seedlings started indoors or in crowded greenhouses—places without enough light—may develop lanky, barren stems that topple over in the garden.

As long as they grow from a single stem (rather than a rosette of leaves) and go into well-drained soil, leggy seedlings can be submerged slightly deep for extra support.

For flexible-stemmed seedlings like tomatoes, a horizontal planting trench is better than a vertical one. It is warmer and better aerated than deeper soil, encouraging good root growth and fast development.

168 **KEEP CUTWORMS AWAY FROM SEEDLINGS** with the cardboard centers of toilet paper rolls—recycling at its best! Cutworms, which are moth caterpillars, creep near the soil surface, eating tender stem bases of young seedlings and cutting sprouts off the roots.

It doesn't take barbed wire or an electric-shock fence to get cutworms to detour away from your seedlings. After planting, just set a 3-inch-long cardboard tube around the seedling. Push the tube down so half is submerged, thus preventing underground attacks. Then once the seedling has grown into a plant, you can remove the cardboard collar.

169 **FOR AN EXTENDED LETTUCE HARVEST,** pick the largest leaves from the outside of the plant and allow the younger inner leaves to continue growing. But when springtime weather begins to get warm, you need to take the opposite strategy. Cut off the entire plant before it begins to send up a flower stem (a condition called bolting) and turns bitter.

170 **PRUNE TOMATO PLANTS** to direct maximum energy into tomato production. Choose your pruning plan based on what you want from your tomatoes. For larger and earlier (but fewer) tomatoes, remove any

EARLY, MIDSEASON, AND LATE TOMATOES

EARLY
'Early Girl'
'Early Pick'
'First Lady'
'Glacier'
'Oregon Spring'

MIDSEASON
'Better Boy'
'Big Beef'
'Big Boy'
'Big Girl'

'Celebrity'
'Delicious'
'Floramerica'
'Heatwave'

LATE
'Homestead'
'Oxheart'
'Wonderboy'
'Supersteak'
'Beefmaster'
'Brandywine'

---

shoots that emerge on or beside the main stem, and tie the stem to a stake. For more tomatoes later, let plants bush out and support them in tomato cages. Pinch off any flowers that open before July 4.

171 CHOOSE BETWEEN DETERMI-NATE AND INDETERMINATE TOMATOES according to the way you prefer to harvest.

Determinate tomatoes (such as 'Celebrity') tend to stay compact and produce most of their tomatoes at about the same time. This is convenient for freezing, canning, and sauce making.

Indeterminate tomatoes (such as 'Big Beef') keep growing and developing new tomatoes as they go. They produce a greater yield spread over a longer harvest period.

Dozens of different cultivars are in each class—plenty to pick from. You might have to check seed catalogues to find out whether a particular tomato is determinate or not.

172 **STAKE YOUR TOMATO CAGES** so a bumper crop won't pull them over. Work a tall stake through the wire mesh near the perimeter of the cage and stab it 4 to 6 inches deep in the ground. This will anchor the cage (and the plant inside) firmly despite the pull of strong winds and branchfuls of ripening tomatoes.

173 **PLANT VERTICALLY TO SAVE SPACE.** Instead of letting beans, cucumbers, melons, and squash sprawl across the ground, you can let them climb up a trellis or arbor.

174 **ADD HEIGHT TO A VEGETABLE GARDEN** with a tepee covered with bean and pea vines. This space saver works similarly to a trellis but has a different look. Make the tepee of six or eight 6-foot-high poles tied together at the top. Plant pole beans, lima beans, or peas around each pole, and they will twine up to the top.

| 175 | **PLANT MORNING GLORY SEEDS AROUND THE STEMS OF SUNFLOWERS.** Lanky sunflowers can look quite barren once the flowers are done blooming. But when clad in morning glories, their beauty lasts for the rest of the growing season.

176 **SIDE-DRESS LONG-GROWING CROPS,** such as indeterminate tomatoes, eggplants, and peppers, with a balanced vegetable-garden fertilizer in order to keep them producing. After the first harvest, sprinkle some granular fertilizer around the perimeter of the plants, then work it lightly into the soil, and water well. The extra nutrients can encourage blossoming of new flowers and development of fruits afterward.

177 **PLANT POTATOES IN RAISED BEDS,** covering them with a little compost-enriched soil. As the potato vines arise, surround them with straw until the layer reaches about 12 inches in thickness. New tubers will develop in the straw, which can be brushed away for a super-simple harvest.

178 **USE NEWSPAPER** covered with straw between garden rows to eliminate weeds and retain moisture. This dynamic duo works more efficiently together than either one alone. At the end of the growing season, rototill the paper and straw into the soil to decay.

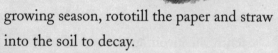

179 **PLANT MELONS AND CUCUMBERS** in the compost pile. (They might grow there anyway if you toss old fruits on the pile in the fall). Warm, moist, nutrient-rich compost seems to bring out the best in melon and cucumber vines.

180 **GET TWICE THE HARVEST** by planting a lettuce and tomato garden in an 18- or 24-inch-wide pot. You can pick the lettuce as it swells and leave extra growing room for the tomatoes. Here's how to proceed:

- ❧ Fill the pot with a premoistened blend of ⅓ compost and ⅔ peat-based potting mix.
- ❧ Plant several leaf lettuce seeds or small seedlings around the edge of the pot and a tomato seedling in the middle.
- ❧ Place the pot in a sunny, frost-free location.
- ❧ Water as needed to keep the soil moist, and fertilize once a month or as needed to encourage good growth.

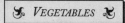

181 **EXTEND THE FALL HARVEST
SEASON** for crops such as cabbage,
Brussels sprouts, and broccoli with a warm
coat of straw. Although it may never be
fashionably chic, straw does trap heat effec-
tively.

Put bales or piles of straw around the
plants, leaving the south side open to the
warm sun. Thus treated, these naturally
frost-tolerant plants may stay in good condition deep into fall, or even into winter in
warmer climates.

CHAPTER 12

HERBS

Herbs are useful for cooking, crafting, and decorating—coming boldly out of the garden into your home. A separate herb garden is wonderful, but herbs can also be blended with flowers and vegetables in a kitchen or a cottage garden. You can also slip herbs in flower or shrub beds, or even into the plantings around your foundation.

Culinary herbs are a mainstay of most herb gardens. The garden-fresh flavors of thyme, basil, savory, oregano, and marjoram are incomparable. You can also grow gourmet varieties of these classics—lemon thyme, cinnamon basil, and Sicilian oregano, for example—to add to your cooking pleasure.

Once your kitchen is well stocked, try lavender and scented geraniums for their sweet perfumes. Add some herbal teas, such as stomach-soothing peppermint and calming chamomile. One of the best and easiest ways to enrich your life is to grow more herbs!

182 **PLAN AN HERB GARDEN** before you plant. Some of the most charming herb gardens have formal beds or geometric patterns that show off the beauty of herbal foliage. Here are some examples:

- ❧ Knot gardens interweave herbs with contrasting leaf color and textures into simple or intricate patterns, many of which are taken from embroidery schemes. Simple knot gardens can be made with two overlapping circles or squares set on a background of mulch or gravel. An easy way to make a knot is with annual herbs such as bush basil, summer savory, or sweet marjoram, or even annual flowers such as French marigolds or ageratum.

❧ Formal herb gardens generally have symmetrical planting plans, with matched herbs on either side of the garden like reflections in a mirror.

❧ Formal and patterned herb gardens often include neat, clipped edgings of boxwood, teucrium, santolina, thyme, winter savory, or other neat herbs suitable for shearing.

183 **PROVIDE SANDY SOIL** for herbs that need well-drained soil of moderate fertility. If kept in soil that's lean and light and drenched in hot sun, these herbs develop excellent flavor and stay free from disease.

If your soil is naturally sandy and well drained, you're in luck. If, instead, it's damp clay, raise the herb garden and add a 3-inch layer of coarse sand and 2 inches of compost to improve drainage. Avoid excessive use of fertilizers, especially those high in nitrogen.

184 **GROW HERBS THAT NEED LIGHT SOIL IN POTS.** When planted in well-drained, peat-based potting mix, herbs such as thyme, lavender, and rosemary thrive— and they look great!

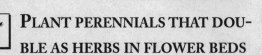

185 **PLANT PERENNIALS THAT DOUBLE AS HERBS IN FLOWER BEDS AND BORDERS.** Some herbs masquerade as perennials (and vice versa) because they can be used for decorating, fragrance, or cuisine. Some examples include the following:

- ❧ Sweetly fragrant bee balm has flowers and foliage wonderful for tea or drying for potpourri.
- ❧ Yarrow bears everlasting flowers for

dried arrangements. Air drying is fine for golden-flowered forms. To preserve the color of pink, red, and white-flowered yarrows, dry them in silica gel.

SOME HERBS FOR LIGHT SOIL

Lavender	Lamb's ears
Sage	Teucrium
Santolina	German chamomile
Thyme	Coriander
Oregano	Hyssop
Sweet fennel	Tarragon
Marjoram	Rosemary
Winter savory	Artemisias
Yarrow	

SOME HERBS FOR MOISTER SOIL

Mints	Lady's mantle
Angelica	Lemon balm
Basil	Parsley
Bee balm	Sorrel
Chives	Sweet woodruff
Horseradish	

- Lady's mantle is a historical herb with lovely scalloped leaves and small sprays of yellow-green flowers for cutting.

- Pinks have fragrant flowers that can be used fresh for cut flower arrangements or dried for potpourri.

186 **USE HERBS WITH ATTRACTIVE FOLIAGE** for season-long color in perennial gardens. Amid the comings and goings of perennial flowers, neatly or color-fully clad herbs maintain enduring style and beauty.

Some of the best herbs to grow for decorative foliage include globe basil (small mounds of emerald green), bronze leaf basil or perilla, ornamental sages (with purple leaves, variegated gold leaves, or tricolor green, white, and pink leaves), and silver-leaved herbs such as gray santolina and lavender.

For a great overall color scheme, complement the color of the foliage with nearby flowers.

187 **PLANT A COLLECTION OF COMMONLY USED CULINARY HERBS** in a

clay planter by a sunny kitchen window. They will be right at hand when you need them.

188 **RESTRAIN RAMPANT HERBS** like mint and bee balm so they can't take over the garden. These plants need firm limits to keep them in their proper place.

Plant rampant herbs in large plastic pots with the bottom removed and the top rim emerging an inch or two above the soil surface. The container will slow down spreading growth enough so you can see trouble before it spills over the edge. Cut back any errant sprouts and use them for tea or to garnish a fruit salad. Divide to renew the chastised plant every year or two.

189 **PINCH BACK ANNUAL HERBS,** such as basil, to keep them from blooming. If allowed to channel energy into seed production, the foliage will grow skimpy and so will your harvest. Pinching off the shoot tips from time to time provides sprigs for herbal vinegars and pestos and inspires the plant to grow back bushier than ever.

190 **REMOVE A FEW BRICKS** in a garden path to make places for low-growing thyme or oregano. Either herb will thrive in this warm, well-drained location and will give a charming natural look and wonderful fragrance to the walkway.

191 **PLANT MORE PARSLEY, DILL, AND FENNEL** than you think you will use to attract swallowtail butterflies. The beauty of the butterflies and fun of watching the caterpillars develop can be worth the foliage that they eat.

192 **HARVEST PERENNIAL HERBS** as they develop flower buds. This is the time when the fragrant and flavorful oils in the plants are at their peak of intensity, providing a gourmet experience. Because fresh herbs taste so good, even at other times of the growing season, it's perfectly acceptable to continue harvesting whenever you feel the urge. In cold climates, however, hardy perennial herbs need a break from heavy harvesting beginning 45 days before the first frost in order to prepare for winter.

CHAPTER 13

FRUITS

S o many different kinds of fruit are available—how do you begin to decide which to grow? Start with quality. When soft berries are homegrown, they can be harvested when fully ripe, plump, and sweet, without concern for shipping and perishability. The flavor is outstanding!

The amount of yard space available will be another deciding factor. Choose between growing small fruits—berries that grow on small plants, vines, or bushes—or larger tree

DISEASE-RESISTANT APPLE CULTIVARS

'Liberty'	'GoldRush'
'Macfree'	'Enterprise'
'Freedom'	'Jonafree'
'Pristine'	

fruits. Start with easily raised, space-efficient small fruits such as strawberries, blackberries, and raspberries. But if you have a place in your landscape for a fruit tree or two, don't pass up the opportunity. Look for easy-care fruit trees, or even nontraditional trees such as mulberries or crabapples.

Traditional orchard trees such as apples, peaches, and pears require some knowledge and attention to pollination, pruning, spraying, fertilizing, and other kinds of care. To minimize or eliminate spraying for disease, look for new disease-resistant cultivars of apple trees.

193 **MULCH STRAWBERRIES** with straw to keep the fruits clean. Straw keeps soil and disease spores, which cause berries to rot and mold, from splashing up onto the berries. As a result, they look nicer and keep longer. Straw also keeps the soil moist, so the berries can plump up, and it helps reduce weeds.

194 **GROW DAY-NEUTRAL STRAWBER-RIES** for a summer-long harvest. While June-bearing strawberries bear fruit heavily in early summer, and ever-bearing strawberries bear in June and again in fall, day-neutrals can keep flowering and fruiting throughout much of the summer.

SOME JUNE–BEARING AND DAY–NEUTRAL STRAWBERRY CULTIVARS

JUNE-BEARING	DAY-NEUTRAL
'Honeoye'	'Tribute'
'Earliglow'	'Tristar'
'Annapolis'	'Fern'
'Redchief'	'Selva'
'Cardinal'	
'Surecrop'	
'Guardian'	
'Lateglow'	

Plant day-neutral strawberries as early in spring as possible and pinch off all the flower buds for six weeks afterward. This lets the plants grow strong before they begin to fruit. Once the plants are flowering, fertilize them monthly to keep the plants vigorous and productive.

Heavy producers such as these may not keep up the pace year after year. When you notice berry production diminishing, consider starting a new strawberry patch with fresh plants.

195 **PLANT STRAWBERRIES IN A STRAWBERRY JAR** for an edible feast on a patio. Strawberry jars stand about two feet high and have openings along the side, perfect for planting with strawberry plants. They look especially charming when little plantlets sprout on runners and dangle down the sides.

Plant in peat-based potting mixed with extra compost. To make watering easier, run a perforated plastic tube down the center of the pot before planting. You can pour

water down the tube to moisten the entire container from the inside out.

196 CUT THE CANES on blackberries and raspberries when first setting out new plants. The canes are the elongated flowering stems. Leave just a few of the leafy buds at the base of the stems. This eliminates any cane diseases that may have hitchhiked to your garden on the plant. It also discourages spring flowering, letting the plant become well established before moving on to berry production.

197 THIN OUT ONE-THIRD OF ALL BLACKBERRY AND RASPBERRY

CANES each year to keep them productive. If you've ever tried to walk through an abandoned farm field bristling with blackberry thickets, you know what a thorny tangle these plants can grow into.

Not only does crowded growth make blackberries and raspberries hard to work around, but it forces canes to compete for sun, nutrients, moisture, and fresh air. The result can be smaller berries and more diseases.

As soon as canes are done bearing fruit, you can cut them off at the base to provide more space for new canes. Remove any sick, weak, or scrawny canes. Then selectively remove additional canes from areas that are crowded or creeping into other parts of the garden.

Pruning is easier if you wear thick, thornproof gloves and use long-handled pruning loppers. A pair of sunglasses to protect your eyes won't hurt either.

198 **PLANT DWARF FRUIT TREES,** which stay small enough for you to pick the fruit from the ground. This is a safe, easy way to harvest. You won't have to lug around ladders or balance on them while working. Another advantage of dwarf fruit trees is they begin to bear fruit much younger than full-sized trees do. And if your lawn is small, a dwarf tree, which takes up less space than its full-size counterpart, is a good alternative.

199 **TRY GROWING A SUPER-DWARF PEACH TREE IN A POT.** Super-dwarfs are extra-miniature trees that may reach only about 5 feet tall. Although other fruit trees come as super-dwarfs, peaches produce flavorful fruit with only one tree and are great for beginners. (Many other fruit trees require a second cultivar for pollination.)

Plant your super-dwarf peach in a 24-inch-wide tub with drainage holes in the bottom. Keep it moist, well fertilized, and in a sunny location during the growing season. If your tree does-n't bear fruit the first year, give it time. It may need another year or two to start its career. During winter in cold climates, store the tree, tub and all, in a cool but protected location.

200 USE STICKY RED BALLS for control of apple maggots on apple and plum trees or blueberry bushes. Apple maggots are fly larvae that tunnel into developing fruit, making it disgusting and inedible.

Apple maggot flies are easily tricked, however. If you put out sticky red balls (homemade or purchased through a garden supply catalog), the egg-laying females will be attracted to the ball and get stuck. (This will end their egg-laying career!) Hang at least one sticky red ball in a dwarf tree and six or more in larger trees.

201 **USE TREE BANDS TO CATCH CRAWLING PESTS** climbing up fruit tree trunks. Sticky plastic bands will catch and hold ants carrying aphids and creeping caterpillars such as gypsy moths and codling moths.

202 **COVER RIPENING BERRIES** with fine netting to keep birds away from them. Birds love the juicy, sweet flavor of berries and begin to be attracted to them as soon as the berries start to color. If the netting is in place, they won't be able to get close enough to do much damage.

CHAPTER 14

ANNUALS AND BIENNIALS

Annuals are flowers that bloom the first year they are planted, often flowering just a couple of months after sowing. Most annuals are started indoors or in greenhouses in late winter or early spring. But when spring frosts are over, plants such as zinnias, nasturtiums, and cosmos can be sown directly in the garden for a summer full of flowers.

In colder climates, tender perennials such as alstroemeria, wax begonia, and some species of impatiens will behave like annuals and must be cultivated as such. These same plants, however, will grow as perennials in their native hot climates.

Biennials like cup and saucer, some foxgloves, and some hollyhocks produce greenery the first year only. During the second year of growth, they flower and set seed destined to become the next generation. If you allow plants to self-sow for at least two years, you will have a steady supply of blooming plants.

203 **RE-CREATE A FAVORITE PATTERN** from a family crest, piece of fabric, or needlepoint with annuals in your flower garden. You've seen similar patterns at amusement parks and public parks. Why not do the same with a pattern that is meaningful to you?

204 **USE PALE SAND TO OUTLINE THE PLANT GROUPINGS** before planting when laying out annual beds. This is like making a pencil sketch of a painting before stroking on the oil paints.

Whether you're planning to put blue ageratums in edging rows, make a teardrop

FRAGRANT ANNUALS

Why not plant some perfumed flowers under an open window or beside the patio? Here are some good choices:

Pinks
Heliotropes
Petunias
Moonflowers
Lemon and Orange Gem marigolds
Fragrant White flowering tobacco
Stocks
Sweet peas

of red zinnias, or create a sweeping mass of pink impatiens, you can adjust and fine-tune the overall shapes before filling them in with colorful flowers. After making the sand outlines, stand back and look at the results objectively. If you don't like the first attempt, cover the sand with soil and try again.

205 PLANT STAGGERED ROWS OF ANNUALS to create a fuller look. A single marching line of annuals such as French marigolds set side by side can look weak in a bigger garden. You can beef up their impact by planting a second row behind the first, with the rear plants centered on the openings between the front-row plants.

Staggered rows are also nice for showcasing taller annuals, such as blue salvia or snapdragons, set in the rear of a garden. A double row of spider flowers can become so full and bushy it resembles a flowering hedge.

206 CHOOSE HEALTHY PLANTS when shopping at the garden center or nursery in spring. Here is a checklist to use before buying any new plant:

- ☙ Leaf color: The foliage of naturally green-leafed plants should be bright green, not faded yellow or scorched bronze or brown.

❧ Plant shape: The sturdiest seedlings will be compact, with short stretches of stem between sets of leaves. Slenderness may be an admirable quality on high-fashion models, but a lanky, skinny seedling is weaker and less desirable than a short, stocky one.

❧ Pests: If you shake the plant, no insects should come fluttering off. Inspect the stem tips and flower buds for aphids, small pear-shaped sap suckers. Look for hidden pests by turning the plant upside down and looking under the leaves and along the stem.

215

Roots: An annual with ideal roots will have filled out its potting soil without growing cramped. When roots are overcrowded, the plant is root-bound— the roots have consumed all soil space and grown tangled and ineffective. The best way to judge root quality is to pop a plant out of its container (or ask a sales clerk to do this) and check to see how matted the roots have become. (Light tangles can be corrected; see Hint 209.)

207 **CHOOSE SHADE-TOLERANT OR SHADE-LOVING ANNUALS** for a lightly shaded garden. Among the annuals that prefer shade are impatiens, browallia, and torenia. Other annuals, the most versatile of the bunch, will grow in sun or light shade. They include wax begonias, sweet alyssum, ageratum, coleus, forget-me-nots, and pansies.

208 **CREATE THE MOST EXCITEMENT**
from your shade garden by choosing
flowers with white, pastel, or brightly colored blossoms. Dark burgundy leaves and
cool blue or purple flowers won't shine the
way brighter blooms do from shady garden
depths.

209 **GENTLY BREAK UP THE ROOT**
BALL of annuals grown in cell packs or
pots before planting them. Often, the roots
have overgrown the potting area and become
matted. You'll have
to pull off the tan-
gles so the roots
will be able to grow
free into the soil.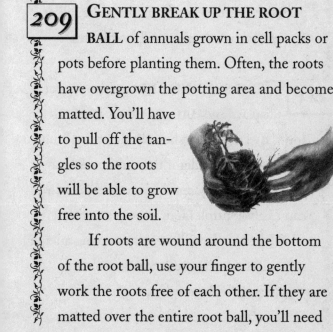

If roots are wound around the bottom
of the root ball, use your finger to gently
work the roots free of each other. If they are
matted over the entire root ball, you'll need

to tear or cut the mats off, leaving the roots below intact.

210 **SNIP BACK LEGGY ANNUALS** when you plant to encourage bushy new growth. Don't hesitate—it's really for the best! Removing the growing tip of a stem stimulates side shoots to sprout, which makes annuals fuller. Since each side shoot can be full of flowers, the whole plant will look better.

211 **USE A SPACING AID** to plant annual displays and cutting gardens in even rows. Even the most beautifully grown annuals can be distracting if they are spaced erratically. Fortunately, spacing is one element you can easily control. Here are some options:

    ❧ Make a planting grid by stapling a large piece of wire mesh over a wooden frame. If the mesh openings are 2 inches square and you want to plant ageratums 6 inches apart, you can put one seedling in every third hole.

- Make a spacing rope. Tie knots in the rope to mark specific measurements, for instance, noting every 4 or 6 inches. You can stretch the rope between two stakes to make even measurements along a straight line.

- Take a yardstick with you when you go to plant. Measure the distance between each plant in a row and between rows rather than simply eyeballing it.

212 **FERTILIZE ANNUALS PERIODI-CALLY** during the growing season to keep them producing. This is particularly helpful after the first flush of blooming flowers begins to fade (which often marks the beginning of a quiet garden during hot summer months).

For best results, deadhead (see Hint 213), then fertilize with a balanced water-soluble or granular fertilizer. A balanced fertilizer contains similar percentages of nitrogen, phosphorus, and potassium. Check the fertilizer package label for application instructions.

213 **REMOVE SPENT BLOSSOMS** from geraniums and other annuals to keep them blooming and tidy. The bigger the flower, the worse it can look when faded, brown, and mushy. Large, globular geranium flowers are particularly prominent when they begin to discolor. Snip off the entire flower cluster. Take off the stem, too, if no other flower buds are waiting to bloom.

This process, called deadheading, is more than mere housekeeping. By removing the old flowers, you prevent seed production, which consumes a huge amount of energy from the plant. Energy saved can be channeled instead into producing new blooms.

214 PINCH ANNUALS like coleus, browallia, and petunias to keep them full. These plants can get tall and gangly as the growing season progresses. A little pinch, removing the top inch or two of stem, will soon correct this problem.

More is at work here than merely shortening the stem. Removing the terminal bud (at the stem tip) allows side branches to grow and make the plant fuller.

215 PLANT NATURALLY SELF-BRANCHING ANNUALS. Your mother may have pinched all her flowers throughout the summer. But many modern types of impatiens, begonias, multiflora petunias, and other annuals have been bred to be self-branching. They stay fuller naturally and may not need any pinching, or at least very little.

216 **TAKE STEM CUTTINGS OF TEN-DER FLOWERS** in late summer before temperatures drop below 50 degrees Fahrenheit. You can root them indoors and enjoy their greenery and perhaps a few flowers during winter. Then you can take more

---

ANNUALS SUITABLE FOR LATE SUMMER CUTTINGS

Geraniums, ivy-leaf
  and standard
Impatiens
Fibrous rooted
  begonias
Coleus

Asters
Petunias
Portulaca
Verbena

---

cuttings of these plants to set out next spring.
Cuttings are more compact and versatile
than old garden plants dug up and squeezed
into a pot. They can thrive with less effort
and space.

Fresh-cut annual stems may root if you
put them in a vase of clean water. But stems
can root more reliably in a sterile, peat-based
mix.

217 **HAVE FLOWERS BLOOMING IN
SUNNY WINDOWS** during fall and
winter by starting new seedlings outdoors in

pots in mid- to late summer.
Bring them indoors several
weeks before the first autumn frost. They will begin
to bloom as frost arrives, perfect
for brightening the autumn transition period. This works well with French
marigolds, pansies, petunias, nasturtiums,

violas, impatiens, compact cockscomb, and annual asters. Simply discard the plants later when they get ratty-looking.

218 **GROW SOME ANNUALS WITH EVERLASTING FLOWERS** to dry for winter arrangements. There are many won-

---

SOME EVERLASTING ANNUALS

COCKSCOMB: plume or comb-shaped flowers in bright red, orange, or yellow

ANNUAL BABY'S BREATH: cloudlike drifts of small white flowers

BELLS OF IRELAND: spikes of green trumpet-shaped flowers

GLOBE AMARANTH: ball-shaped flowers of white, pink, purple, and orange

LOVE-IN-A-MIST: maroon-striped seed pods

STATICE: bright sprays of pink, purple, yellow, white, and blue flowers

STRAWFLOWERS: double daisylike flowers with straw-textured petals in red, pink, white, gold, and bronze

---

derful annuals to choose from. Those listed on page 224 are easily dried if spread out in a warm, dark, airy place.

If seedlings of everlasting annuals are not available at your local garden center, consider starting your own seedlings indoors (see Hint 93).

219 **RELIVE A LITTLE SLICE OF HISTORY** by growing a few heirloom flowers. These are flowers your ancestors may have enjoyed. Many of these plants are returning to popularity, thanks to their interesting appearances. Some heirlooms are only slightly different from modern flowers—taller, larger- or smaller-flowered, or more fragrant. But other heirlooms are quite distinct and unusual. Here are some examples:

🌶 Love-lies-bleeding: Long, dangling, crimson red seed heads form colorful streamers.

- Kiss-me-over-the-garden-gate: These six-foot-tall plants have pendulous pink flowers.
- Balsam: This impatiens relative sprinkles flowers amid the foliage along the stems.
- Sweet peas: Vining pea-shaped plants that bear colorful pink, white, purple, and red flowers with delightful fragrances.

220 **IN INFORMAL GARDENS, PLANT NONHYBRID ANNUALS** that may return from self-sown seeds allowed to mature and fall to the ground. Suitable annuals include the heirlooms love-lies-bleeding and kiss-me-over-the-garden-gate; wildflowers such as cornflowers, California poppies, and verbenas; and open-pollinated annuals such as snapdragons, portulaca, cockscomb, and spider flowers.

CHAPTER 15

PERENNIALS

Perennials are distinct from annuals in that they return year after year, eliminating the need to buy new flowers every spring. Unlike annuals, perennials generally bloom only one or, at the most, two seasons per year. There are spring bloomers, summer bloomers, or fall bloomers. When they're not in flower, perennials are enjoyed for their foliage, which is at least as important a consideration as the blooms.

Perennial shapes and sizes also add to the mix. There are tall perennials like plume poppy that tower over your head and creeping perennials like moss phlox that carpet the ground.

Perennials may grow and expand each year, eventually filling more space than you might expect. To keep perennials under control and growing well, many need division (digging up the root clump, dividing it into sections, and replanting the best sections in freshened soil). This can provide a harvest of new plants for use elsewhere in the garden.

221 **ARRANGE THE PERENNIAL GAR-DEN** so that you can see and enjoy every plant—regardless of how small it is. Place the tallest plants in the rear of a border that is viewed exclusively from the front. In an island bed viewed from all sides, place tall plants in the middle.

Work medium-height plants into the middle of a border or island bed, filling out the garden in front of the taller plants. Set small plants up front, where they won't be hidden by taller leaves or flowers.

The neat progression of short to tall gives a garden a sense of order and tidiness many people appreciate. Don't be too rigid, however. You can work some medium-size varieties into the plants up front to add interest (see Hint 222).

222 **BRING A FEW TALL PLANTS FOR-WARD** to break up any tendency to make height organization rigid. A garden can look more natural and interesting if it's allowed a few height variations. Here are some ideas to try (also see Hint 223):

- ❧ Plant some medium-height early bloomers such as columbines toward the front of the garden. They will flower before the other perennials are stirring and can be cut back after flowering so that only compact leaves remain.

- ❧ Swing an arc of medium-height plants up toward the front of the border, making a gentle curve that softens height restrictions but doesn't

extend so far into the front of the
border that it becomes restrictive.

🍃 Loop a small drift of shorter edging
plants back into the medium-height
flower section to ease the dividing
line between the two.

223 **USE PLANTS WITH AIRY SPRAYS
OF SMALL FLOWERS** at the front of
the garden. Perennials like baby's breath and
coral bells have see-through veils of blossoms
that don't obscure what's behind them. This
can make the garden sparkle.

224 **COMBINE SEVERAL DIFFERENT
PERENNIAL FORMS** to keep the garden from being monotonous. Diversity
provides spice to perennial gardening.

Many perennials fall into the following
shape categories. But you should expect
variations as the seasons progress. Perennials

usually stretch up to flower and then fade back to their foliage after the bloom is through.

🌿 Mats: Perennials such as lamium, bugle-  weed, and plumbago form low carpets suitable for ground covers or the front of the border.

🌿 Mounds: Nicely rounded perennials such as coreopsis and hostas provide a soft look.

🌿 Flower sprays with low foliage: Perennials such as yarrow, sea thrift, and coral bells bear taller flowers over neat low foliage. Height is dramatically reduced when the old flower stems are removed.

🌿 Vase shapes: When in bloom, plants such as garden phlox and Shasta daisies grow in an inverted triangular shape.

◆ Spikes: Plants such as salvias, lupines, gayfeathers, and delphiniums have slim, vertical flowering stems that contrast well with more horizontal forms.

225 **CHOOSE HEALTHY PLANTS.** For the inexperienced buyer, this may be easier said than done in the spring. Potted perennials may be showing only a little foliage, not providing much information about the health of the plant. Here are a few things you can do to get a better picture:

◆ Look at the plant crown, the place where the shoots emerge from the soil. The emerging stems and leaves should be nicely

232

green and showing no sign of wilting
or rotting.

🍃 Study the foliage and soil surface for
signs of pests, which might be feeding on the crown, beneath the leaves,
or fluttering up when you move the
pot. If you find extensive evidence of
pests, buy your plants elsewhere.

🍃 Ask a sales clerk if you can look at
the plant roots. Turn the pot over
and slip the root ball out. The roots
should fill the pot, but not be
crammed into it, and they should
be healthy and firm.

226 **KEEP YOUR EXPECTATIONS FOR
PLANT LIFE REALISTIC.** Although
perennials like daylilies and hostas can live
for decades, some perennials live only a few
years. Perennials with short-but-sweet lives
include columbine, blanketflower, and some

PERENNIALS WITH WIDE-RANGING FLOWER COLORS

DAYLILIES: pink, yellow, red, purple, cream

IRIS: purple, red, yellow, white, blue

LUPINES: yellow, red, pink, orange, blue

LILIES: pink, red, white, yellow

POPPIES: pink, red, white, cream, orange

PHLOX: pink, orange, purple, white, blue

POTENTILLA: pink, white, red, yellow

PEONIES: white, pink, red, yellow

chrysanthemums. Propagate new plants using division, cuttings, or seed to have replacements ready when needed. (See Chapter 7, "Propagation," for more detailed instructions.)

227 **AVOID WILDFLOWERS COLLECTED IN THE WILD.** Some people snatch wildflowers from native areas instead of

propagating them in a nursery. This depletes
the natural environment and can result in
inferior plants not prepared for garden life.
Buy from a reputable garden center or nursery. Ask where they got the wildflowers and
whether they were nursery propagated.

Be suspicious if you see pots with several small plants packed irregularly, which
may have been taken from the wild. Flowers
that are poorly rooted may have been recently dug and stuck in a pot. If you see
wildflowers sold for less than a comparable
perennial, it's a sign that they may have been
harvested in the wild.

228 CHOOSE SINGLE-FLOWERED
PEONIES over the double-flowered
types. A single-flowered plant has a solitary
row of petals (or several rows, in the case of
peonies) around the perimeter of each blos-
som. Double-flowered plants have many

rows of petals, which
form a full, fluffy-look-
ing flower.

The big advantage of
single-flowered peonies is
weight. With fewer petals, the
flowers stay lighter and are less likely to fall
over when in full bloom. This means they
don't need staking. The flowers are also less
likely to trap moisture and, consequently,
tend to suffer from fewer diseases.

229 **PLAN AHEAD TO COVER THE
GAPS** left by perennials that go dormant in summer. Two of the most common
now-you-see-them-now-you-don't perennials are sun-loving, Oriental poppies and
shade-loving, old-fashioned bleeding hearts.
When done blooming, both plants slough
off their old foliage and hibernate underground. This creates vacant places in the

garden. But with a little planning, you can easily work around them.

- Plant Oriental poppies or bleeding hearts individually instead of in large clumps or drifts, which leave larger holes.

- Organize gardens so that neighboring plants can fill in and cover for the missing greenery. In shade, the ample foliage of hostas and ferns can move into voids left when old-fashioned bleeding hearts go dormant. In sun, hardy geraniums, frothy baby's breath flowers, and spreaders like dragon's blood sedum can fill in for Oriental poppies.

- Set a potted plant, such as a houseplant spending the summer outdoors, temporarily in the opening.

230 **CHOOSE DISEASE-RESISTANT CULTIVARS** of garden phlox and bee balm. Both perennials can be troubled with mildew diseases, which cover the plants with ugly white fuzz. Fortunately, developing disease-resistant cultivars has become a priority in the nursery industry. Check perennial catalogues to identify the best new cultivars for your climate.

231 **SOAK BARE-ROOT PERENNIALS** in a bucket of water for an hour before planting. Bare roots have been out of their element (moist soil) while handled and shipped. Letting them soak up a little extra moisture can refresh moisture levels so the roots can grow vigorously in the weeks ahead.

232 **MOLD THE PLANTING HOLE** to provide the proper support for a bare-root perennial. When planting potted perennials, the shape of the pot is a good match for the hole you dig. But bare-root perennials tend to have octopuslike roots that need different treatment.

- ❧ Dig a wide, shallow hole in well-prepared soil.
- ❧ Form a cone of soil in the center of the hole. Make the cone high enough to hold the crown (where the shoots emerge from the roots) at the soil surface.
- ❧ Spread the roots around the perimeter of the cone so that each has its own space. The hole should be deep enough

to accommodate the entire root length without a lot of cramming, twisting, and turning.

🌿 Fill in around the roots with soil, and keep it moist.

233 **SHAKE THE POTTING MIX** off the roots of potted perennials and plant them like bare-root perennials. Larger perennials sold in 1- or 2-quart-size containers are perfect candidates for this. The reason for doing this is that peat potting mixes can complicate plant establishment in the soil. The roots of perennials grown in peat-based mixes can have difficulty growing out of the peat and into the native soil. In addition, peat can quickly become parched in drying soils, causing root damage. Getting the peat out eliminates both of these problems and can help new perennials get established faster than you ever thought possible.

234 **START A SHADE GARDEN UNDER TREES** by adding 4 inches of compost over the tree roots before planting. Rich, moist compost provides a fast start for newly planted perennials. This is important—the flowers need to be growing strongly before tree roots move in and capitalize on their growing space. Compost also helps keep the garden moist in summer, when the trees and perennials may compete for water. Just be careful when planting not to damage the tree roots.

235 **USE PLANTS ADAPTED TO DRY CONDITIONS IN DROUGHT-PRONE CLIMATES.** Perennials such as butterfly weed have deep or moisture-storing roots that allow them to weather dry conditions. Other drought-survival specialists have leaves that are modified to reduce moisture loss. Silver leaves reflect hot sun-

DROUGHT–TOLERANT PERENNIALS

Yarrow	Purple coneflower
Artemisia	Gayfeather
Butterfly flower	Lavender
Sea pink	Russian sage
Orange coneflower	Sedum

light, and needle-shaped leaves have less surface area for moisture loss. Moisture is stored inside succulent leaves, and moisture loss for furry leaves is slowed by their furry coating.

236 **SPACE LARGE, SLOW-GROWING PERENNIALS PROPERLY** at the start. Big hostas, goat's beard, gas plants, and roses, for example, can be hard to move once they are established. Ask at the nursery or check in a garden encyclopedia for information on how big the plant will get. Then be sure to allow enough space for the plant to reach its mature limits without overcrowding.

237 **AVOID DENSE TREE ROOTS** by planting a shade garden around the outside of the tree canopy rather than directly underneath. Many tree roots cluster under the branch canopy, and active feeding goes on near the drip line, the place where rainwater drips off the leafy branch tips. Gardening beyond the shadow of the limbs reduces root competition, and the plants will get more light.

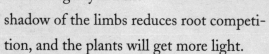

238 **CONVERT YOUR FRONT YARD TO A COTTAGE GARDEN.** Tending flowers is much more fun than mowing grass!

239 **PLANT SHADE-LOVING PERENNI-
ALS ON THE SHADY NORTH SIDE
OF SHRUBS** if you don't have trees. Perennials
such as anemones, astilbes, hostas, Lenten
roses, and violets can look lovely against a
backdrop of evergreen shrubs. Flowering
deciduous shrubs such as viburnums or
hydrangeas can be even more beautiful.

240 **MAKE AN ARTIFICIAL BOG** for
plants that need constantly wet soil.
Then you will be able to grow swamp irises,
variegated cattails, ligularias, and other
water-loving
plants.

Begin by
deciding where
you want the bog
garden to be located. They are natural com-
panions for fountains, water gardens, bridges,
or streams. Dig out a deep trench or swale

for the bog garden, then line the hole with plastic. Set a perforated hose in the bottom, with an end emerging from one side to connect with your household hose. Fill the hole with rich soil and plant bog natives. You can irrigate through the submerged hose as needed to keep the garden constantly moist.

241 **INTERPLANT PERENNIALS WITH RESEEDING ANNUALS** for a lush look that changes every year. For more on these annuals, see Hint 220.

242 **PLANT PERENNIALS INSTEAD OF GRASS** in the boulevard strip. The boulevard strip is the very public space located between the sidewalk and the road. It can be hot, dry, and heavily trod upon, which makes it difficult to keep grass looking healthy and nice.

Instead of fighting a constant battle

with turf, use a different tactic. Plant the boulevard strip with low but bushy perennials that people won't walk on. Choose heat- and drought-tolerant perennials such as coreopsis, 'Silver Mound' artemisia, and sea thrift. Now the problem area can become a pretty garden.

243 **USE SALT-TOLERANT PERENNIALS** in cold-climate roadside plantings. Roads heavily salted during winter snowstorms often leave salt residue in the soil. Perennials such as sea thrifts, bearberry, and rugosa roses thrive in soils that are salty enough to kill other plants.

244 **LESSEN THE IMPACT OF WIND** by planting tall perennials and ornamental grasses to shelter a garden full of more delicate plants. Sturdy-stemmed perennials, which are not likely to topple over with the first big gust, grow large enough to curb the wind faster than most shrubs and trees. Some perennials to try are maiden grasses, pampas grass, boltonia, goat's beard, and large hostas.

This tip also works on a smaller scale. You can plant smaller, delicate flowers beside sturdy medium-sized plants like purple coneflowers and irises for wind protection.

245 **SUPPORT FULL, FLOPPY PERENNIALS WITH PRUNED TWIGS.** This is an old British trick called pea staking. It helps perennials stay upright and look natural without glaring metallic stakes or forced shapes that result from corseting with twine. Even better, pea staking costs nothing but a little time.

When the perennials begin to arise in spring, set the ends of sturdy branched twigs around the plant. The twigs should be about

as long as the height of the perennial. As the stems grow, they will fill out to hide the twigs. You can cut off any errant woody stems that remain in sight after the perennial reaches full height.

246 **PLANT TALL PERENNIALS TOGETHER** so they can support each other without any staking. Combinations such as boltonia and asters, yarrows and butterfly weed, or daisies and irises can result in pretty blends of flowers and foliage.

247 **AVOID OVERFERTILIZING** sun-loving prairie plants like coneflowers, yarrows, and coreopsis. Excess fertilizer stimulates taller growth, making these plants more likely to weaken and flop over.

248 PINCH ASTERS AND MUMS.

Pinching is one of the handiest things you can do in the garden (see Hint 214). Removing the stem tip, with a pinch of your fingernails or with pruning shears, makes plants more compact and bushy.

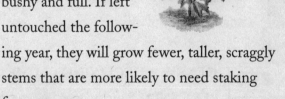

Pinching is particularly helpful for mums and asters. Flowering plants purchased in a pot have been specially treated to make the plants bushy and full. If left untouched the following year, they will grow fewer, taller, scraggly stems that are more likely to need staking for support.

When pinching, scheduling is important. You want to start early enough to make an impact. And you need to stop by July 1 so flower buds can develop before heavy cold strikes. Start with this pinching schedule but feel free to modify it as you gain experience:

- Pinch shoot tips when the stems are 4 to 6 inches high.
- Pinch again three weeks later.
- Pinch a final time in late June.

249 **SHEAR REBLOOMING PERENNI- ALS** such as catmint and 'moonglow' coreopsis to promote a second flush of flowers. Getting rid of the old flowers and seed pods encourages new growth, new buds, and new flowers. This is a great reward for a small amount of effort.

250 **RENEW A DECLINING CLUMP OF PERENNIALS** by division. As many perennials grow, new shoots emerge at the perimeter of the clump, spreading outward. The center becomes older—sometimes woody, sometimes completely barren.

The solution is division. In spring, late summer, or fall, dig up the entire clump. Cut out the old heart, refresh the soil with organic matter, and replant healthy young pieces. (Also see Hints 106 and 107.) You may have enough good divisions left to share with friends.

251 USE A STRING TRIMMER to cut back ornamental grasses in spring. The golden leaves and seed plumes are a great winter attraction. But in spring, the old growth must be removed before the new shoots begin to sprout. The string trimmer quickly cuts through grass stems. Rake them up and toss them on the compost pile—job finished!

252 | **MAKE PLANTERS OUT OF OLD TREE STUMPS** that are next to your house in a mixed border amid a grove of shade trees or in a woodland edge. In nature, old stumps slowly begin to decay and provide fertile places for ferns and other interesting small plants to grow.

You could plant flora native to your area or fill the opening with brightly colored annual flowers and vines.

Benefits include: You won't have to pay to have the stump ground out; you can grow plants that need good drainage or special soil mixes right in the trunk; and you create an interesting, sculpturelike structure.

Chip some wood out of the top of the stump to create rooting space. Fill with a soil mix that's appropriate for the plants you intend to grow. Keep the soil moist.

BULBS

When winter finally melts away, crocuses, daffodils, and tulips are quick to appear. The earliest spring bloomers come from bulbs and other allied structures such as tubers, rhizomes, and corms, which lie underground ready to grow as soon as the weather breaks.

When planted in a compatible site, daffodils, snowdrops, and crocuses can spread into large clusters that paint the landscape with their early color. Long-stemmed tulips and daffodils are wonderful flowers to cut and bring indoors. Hyacinths, dwarf irises, and some daffodils have sweet fragrances, making them pleasurable indoors or out.

Summer is made more cheerful with brightly colored summer-flowering bulbs such as caladiums, dahlias, cannas, and gladioli. These bulbs are native to warmer climates and won't survive winter in cold areas. But they can be dug up, stored in the basement, and replanted when warm weather returns.

When heat has other plants resting, summer-flowering bulbs can continue to thrive. Their bountiful blooms make splendid bouquets.

253 **PLANT SPRING-FLOWERING BULBS** to give early seasonal color to lifeless perennial beds. While the perennials are just beginning to stir and arise, the bulbs are decked with color. As the bulbs are fading, the perennials are beginning to come on strong. It is an ideal partnership.

254 **PLAN AHEAD TO FIND THE BEST PLACE** for interplanting bulbs with perennials. Although they bloom in the spring, early flowering bulbs must be planted in the fall. They look best set in clumps around or between perennials such as hardy geraniums, daylilies, and Siberian irises that don't need frequent division (which would disrupt the bulbs).

Don't wait until the bulbs arrive in October. Mark ideal planting places with a tag or stake in spring or summer, when your existing bulbs are blooming and clumps of perennials are still small. Later in the autumn, when the perennials are dormant, you'll already have the best planting places marked.

255 | **CHOOSE HEALTHY BULBS.** Use the same criteria you would use if shopping for good-quality onions in the grocery store.

 ❧ Look for plump bulbs without soft spots or dark, diseased blotches.

- Check the basal plate, where the roots will emerge. It should be firm and un-damaged.

- Daffodil bulbs with two noses will provide twice the bloom, but tulip bulbs should have only one nose. With two noses, tulip bulbs won't flower.

256 **COMBINE BULB ORDERS WITH YOUR FRIENDS** to buy wholesale and save money. One bulb catalog sells 100 tulip bulbs for just a few dollars more than 50 tulip bulbs. You should order early to get the best selection and prompt delivery.

257 **SOAK FALL-PLANTED BULBS** for 12 hours in warm water before planting. This moisturizing method works with tuni-cate-type bulbs (neatly enclosed round or teardrop-shaped bulbs) and is not suitable for lily or other bulbs with loose, fleshy scales. Soaking allows suitable bulbs to absorb enough water to begin growth immediately, saving two or three weeks of time. This is  particularly helpful in northern climates, where early-arriving winter weather limits leisurely rooting.

258 **ADD LIQUID RODENT REPELLENT** to bulb-soaking water (at the lowest recommended concentration) to make the treated bulbs unappetizing to rodents.

Bitter-tasting rodent repellent is absorbed by the bulbs, which then become unattractive to mice, chipmunks, rabbits, raccoons, skunks, and most other animals. It's particularly helpful for crocuses and other edible, shallowly planted bulbs that are easily unearthed and eaten by passing critters.

259 **PLANT A DOUBLE LAYER** of 'Paper White' narcissus bulbs for twice the flower display. 'Paper White' narcissus, with sweetly scented clusters of small, white daffodil flowers, are warm-climate bulbs that naturally bloom during winter. Pot them in late fall or early winter, and then watch them come to life in a sunny window, even as the snow falls outside.

Most people plant five or six bulbs in an 8-inch bulb pot or forcing dish, which makes a nice enough display. But if you can find a deeper nursery pot, you can plant a bottom and top layer of bulbs to produce awe-inspiring results.

> ❧ Put several inches of moist, peat-based potting mix in the bottom of a deep pot.
> ❧ Set bulbs in the mix, with the flat root-

ing plate down and the pointed nose up. Put the bulbs side by side around the perimeter of the pot and fill the center with one or several bulbs (the number will vary depending on the size of the pot).

- Cover the lower-level bulbs with an inch or two of moist potting mix.
- Set the upper layer of bulbs in this mix, positioning them between (not over) the sprouting noses of the lower-level bulbs.
- Cover the upper level with potting mix, allowing any lanky green sprouts to emerge uncovered.
- Set the potted bulbs in a cool location to root for several weeks. Keep the pot moist but not wet. Then bring the pot into a warm, sunny window and let the growth begin!

260 **PLANT A TRIPLE LAYER OF BULBS**
in the garden. The technique is similar
to that in Hint 259 but the characters differ.

The idea here is to have a shallowly
planted layer of early bloomers like crocuses,
snowdrops, or squills for early spring color.
Just below them, planted about 5 or 6 inches
deep, put daffodils that bloom in mid-spring.
Underneath the daffodils, plant late-bloom-
ing tulips, which benefit from deep planting
and finish up the flower display. You can also
plant up a large pot in the same fashion for a
burst of early color.

261 **MAKE INTENSIVE BULB PLANT-
INGS WORK SMOOTHLY** (see Hint
260) by discouraging competition or disease
spread. Use only well-drained soil for bulbs
(see Hint 6). In wet soils, bulbs will rot. Plan
to fertilize in the fall with a product formulated for bulbs so they won't have to compete

for nutrients. Water during spring while bulbs are actively growing, but allow the soil to dry out in summer, when they are dormant.

262 **DISCOURAGE RODENTS FROM EATING CROCUSES** and other bulbs by planting them in fine-mesh wire baskets.

If animals can't dig the bulbs out, they can't eat them. Wire 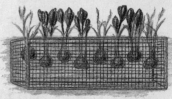 cages also help prevent accidental human damage with shovels and hoes.

BULBS NOT PRONE TO RODENT ATTACKS

Squills
Flowering onions
Colchicums (autumn bloomers)
Crown imperial
Daffodils (narcissus); also called jonquils

263 **PLANT TULIPS 8 TO 10 INCHES DEEP** to prolong their life and protect

them from ro-
dents. When set
deep, tulip bulbs
are slower to split
and stop flowering.

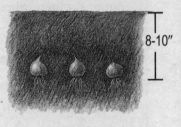

8-10"

They also take some serious digging to be
reached by rodents. It's a win-win situation.

264 **PLANT THE SAME CULTIVAR OF DAFFODIL TOGETHER** in groups of
10, 20, or more. Then all the flowers will
bloom together—at the same time, in the
same color—making a maximum impact.
Just a few daffodils look lonely, and a clump
of mixed colors and cultivars looks chaotic.

265 **DIVIDE OR FERTILIZE CROWDED DAFFODILS** to increase their bloom.
Daffodils that have multiplied to form a

large clump may have depleted the soil nutrients and riddled all the rooting space in the process. The result may be plenty of green leaves but few or no flowers. The solution is as easy as fertilizer or as down-to-earth as division.

Start by applying fertilizer. Slow-release bulb fertilizers can be used in fall for good root growth and continued effectiveness in early spring. Or you can use an all-purpose, balanced fertilizer when growth begins in the spring.

To divide daffodils, dig up the bulbs as the foliage fades. Separate old and new bulbs, refresh the soil with organic matter, and replant with generous spacing.

266 **REMOVE THE BULBILS** from the stems of lilies and plant them to make new plants. These bulbils, or secondary bulbs, look like small, dark berries but con-

tain no seeds at all. They
are similar to miniature
bulbs and have the ability
to sprout into new plants.
Give them a chance, and
watch them grow.

267 **CUT LILY STEMS TO THE GROUND**
in fall to avoid stem rot. It's better to be
safe than sorry!

268 **MARK THE LOCATION OF BULBS**
with a stake, stick, rock, or tag so you
know where they are while they're dormant.
Without an above-ground reminder, it's easy
to dig into the bulbs by mistake when planting
other flowers or vigorously hoeing out weeds.

269 **COVER LARGE PATCHES OF BULBS**
with a ground cover that will fill the
void when the bulbs go dormant. Bulbs

brighten the ground cover in spring, and the ground cover helps keep the bulbs cool and dry in summer. You may need to fertilize more often since twice the amount of plants will be growing in the same space.

270 **CUSTOMIZE BULBS AND GROUND COVERS** by considering their height, sturdiness, and foliage thickness.

Bulbs with weak stems cannot emerge through heavy-leafed ground covers such as pachysandra. Small-leafed ground covers with more open growth, such as periwinkle, can be more suitable.

Bulbs must be tall enough to grow up and over any ground cover surrounding them. Short, early spring bloomers like crocuses may be better placed with deciduous ground covers like epimedium (which die back to the ground in winter) than with evergreen ground covers like ivy.

271 **LEAVE BULB FOLIAGE LOOSE** to ripen properly. Cutting off the foliage before it yellows severs bulbs' food supply and weakens them. Putting daffodils in bondage by tying up their leaves also reduces food production and makes them more prone to disease attack. Taking care of bulb

SOME TULIPS WITH HANDSOME, COLORED FOLIAGE

GREIGII TULIPS
'Donna Bella'
'Red Riding Hood'
'Grand Prestige'
'Margaret Herbst'
'Oratorio'

SPECIES TULIPS
Tulipa linifolia
Tulipa maximowiczii

FOSTERIANA TULIPS
'Easter Moon'
'Juan'

KAUFMANNIANA TULIPS
'Showwinner'
'Johann Strauss'

foliage, even though the bloom is gone, helps ensure more flowers in the years to come.

272 **CUT THE TALL, SPENT STEMS OF TULIP FLOWERS** down to the first leaf. This removes the old flower, an important task called deadheading (see Hint 213). It also leaves the attractive broad foliage to ripen in the garden as nature intended.

273 **BRIGHTEN UP DULL SPOTS IN THE GARDEN** with pots of tender bulbs such as agapanthus, tuberous begonias, caladiums, pineapple lilies, or tuberoses. The versatility of pots combined with the bright blooms of summer-flowering bulbs keeps gardens looking exceptional all summer and fall.

274 **STORE TENDER BULBS IN VERMI-CULITE OR PEAT** to keep them from drying out. These materials are a packing cushion and more. They help keep the bulbs from drying out and rotting. Peat moss, which is naturally disease-resistant, is particularly good for this job.

- Dig the bulbs when the soil is relatively dry so they won't emerge caked with mud. Follow the timing recommended in Hints 277 and 278.

- Gently brush off any extra soil, and remove any old vegetation. Throw out any damaged bulbs.

- Prepare a place for winter storage. Place a layer of vermiculite or peat in the bottom of a plastic storage box. Use one kind of bulb per box or one kind per layer, making sure to label each layer so you know which is which next spring.

- Set the bulbs in the peat or vermiculite, keeping bulbs an inch or two away from each other.

- Cover with a thick layer of peat or vermiculite and add another group of bulbs, repeating this process until all are packed.

- Store in a cool, but not cold, place during winter.

- Check the bulbs at least once a month (preferably more often). Remove any that may have rotted. If all the bulbs begin to shrivel, dampen the packing medium slightly to prevent further moisture loss.

275 **DIVIDE DAHLIAS** to make more plants every year. Dahlias contain underground food-storing rhizomes—a modified form of stem that looks a little like a potato.

The rhizomes connect to a central stalklike crown, which contains all the growth buds. Look closely to find the small scaly bumps or sprouts that indicate where a new shoot will arise. Both rhizomes and shoots are necessary for a new division to succeed.

In the spring, take dahlia rhizomes out of storage. Cut the crown longitudinally into several pieces, each with at least one rhizome and growth bud. Now each division can act as an independent plant.

276 **PRESTART DAHLIAS INDOORS** six weeks before the last spring frost arrives so you can have extra-early flowers.

- Plant the tubers in large nursery pots filled with compost-enriched peat-based potting mix.
- Put the pots in a warm, bright location. The plants will begin rooting and sprouting.

● Dahlias can stay in large pots all summer, as long as you keep the soil moist and add extra fertilizer. Or you can transplant them outdoors into the garden when the danger of spring frosts pass.

277 **DIG COLD-SENSITIVE TROPICAL BULBS** such as cannas and caladiums before the first fall frost to prevent damage to the bulbs. Damaged bulbs are likely to rot in winter storage.

278 **DIG COLD-TOLERANT TENDER BULBS** such as dahlias and gladioli after a light frost has killed the foliage.

279 **POINT THE SHOVEL BLADE**—not the handle—straight down into the soil when digging bulbs. This prevents the shovel from angling into nearby bulbs and slicing them in half.

CHAPTER 17

GROUND COVERS AND VINES

Ground covers spread across barren patches of soil, coating them with greenery. Some ground covers offer a tapestry of both colorful flowers and foliage. The varying colors, heights, and textures contrast with the nearby lawn, highlighting the shape of the ground-cover bed.

Some ground covers also grow where no grass can thrive. In shady areas under trees, dead nettle and periwinkles are at home. On steep banks, where lawn mowing is difficult, great-looking daylilies or junipers can grow thickly enough to stop erosion. Some also double as vines, growing vertically as easily as horizontally. They can even blend tree trunks, walls, and fences into the scenery with a patina of greenery.

Other vines may have flowers, colorful foliage, or fruit that make them spectacular vertical accents to train on a fence, trellis, or lamppost. Some climb freely by twining or with tendrils. Others, like climbing roses, need your assistance to assure their secure ascendance.

280 **ADD HEIGHT TO A PERENNIAL BORDER** with annual or perennial vines on wire cages, tepees, or scrims. When you want a dynamic high point for a flower garden, an upward-trained vine will be effective throughout the growing season and sometimes beyond. In contrast, many of the tallest perennials reach their maximum height only when in flower, which may last for just a few weeks. Here are some support options to consider:

🍃 Wire cages: These work like tomato cages but can be made from wire mesh in

273

any height or shape. A narrow, upright pillar shape is elegant in a formal garden.

❧ Tepees: Make a support of angled posts tied together at the top. Plant one or several vines at the base and let them twine up and fill out to cover the post (see Hint 174).

❧ Scrims: These are open-structured, see-through supports that vines can climb and still provide a veiled view of the scene beyond. With imagination, scrims can be made of braided wire or other creative materials.

281 **CREATE SUMMER SHADE** on a porch with a string trellis covered with vines. String trellises, available from garden centers or mail-order garden catalogues, can be hung from a roof or held upright with posts. Set the trellis to the south or west side of the porch to block the most sun.

282 USE A WIRE TRELLIS AND VINES to cover a blank, dull wall or a utility pipe. A trellis-covered wall comes to life with greenery. Just make sure the trellis is far enough away from the wall; a trellis snug against a wall is not good for either the building or the vines. If you are screening a utility pipe, be sure to leave access openings for maintenance.

283 PIN PERENNIAL VINES LIKE CLIMBING HYDRANGEA TO THE WALL to help them get started. Check a complete garden supply catalog or garden center for various hooks and loops that can be set into your wall to start vines out.

In the beginning, climbing hydrangea might set off in any direction, so guiding it in the right direction is worthwhile. Once it has started, climbing hydrangea ascends by clinging and is well able to scale solid walls or tree trunks.

284 **USE VINES TO COVER** a chain-link fence or other backyard eyesores. They can screen off your garage from view (or your neighbor's garage), make a hidden alcove for your garbage cans, or cover a barren-trunked tree or a fenced dog run. Remember to plant vines that twine or have tendrils on open supports like chain-link fencing and vines that climb on solid supports like walls.

285 **USE VINES TO MAKE A DEAD TREE DISAPPEAR** into a mass of blooms. Just as grapevines in the woods can cover trees and turn them into a dripping mass of green vines, an old stump can become a garden pillar.

In mild climates, ever-
green vines can provide reliable cover year-round. In cold

HOW DIFFERENT VINES CLIMB

**TWINING: NEED SOMETHING TO
TWIST AROUND**
Kiwi
Bougainvillea
Bittersweet
Morning glory
Honeysuckle
Wisteria
Black-eyed Susan vine

TENDRILS: NEED SUPPORT TO GRASP
Clematis
Passion flowers
Grapes

CLINGING: CAN STICK TO SOLID OBJECTS
Ivy
Climbing hydrangea
Trumpet creeper
Wintercreeper
Virginia creeper

climates, some evergreen vines can be more prone to dieback when temperatures really drop. Look for extra-hardy vines for this job.

286 **PLANT VINES ON AN OPEN PERGOLA FRAME** to create a cool, shaded retreat. A pergola is an arborlike structure with an overhead trellis that forms a garden roof. It can make a shady place to sit outside in summer and give the garden elegant architecture at the same time.

To fill out the roof with foliage and flowers, try planting vines that have abundant growth, so they will be well able to go the distance needed. Some possibilities are wisteria, silver fleece vine, kiwi vine, hops, and grapes.

287 **TRY AN EXTRA-EASY WAY TO SUPPORT ANNUAL VINES** with a trellis made from biodegradable twine. Set two 4-

GROUND COVER FOR SHADY PLACES

Boston ivy
Virginia creeper
Periwinkle
Wintercreeper
Lily-of-the-valley
Dead nettle
Sedges
Wild ginger

Golden star
Epimedium
Sweet woodruff
Pachysandra
Woodland phlox
Hardy geraniums
(some species)

foot-high posts about 4 feet apart, pounding their bases about 10 inches deep into the ground. Run the twine between the posts, knotting it around the posts occasionally to keep the twine from slipping down. You may want to make vertical webbing by working the twine up and down between horizontal strands, which helps some vines climb more efficiently.

Plant annual vines such as sweet peas, cardinal climbers, or black-eyed Susan vines beneath the new trellis, and allow them to grow and cover it. When frost arrives or the vines begin to look shabby, simply cut off the twine trellis and throw it, vines and all, in the compost pile.

288 **PLANT GROUND COVER IN POCK-ETS OF SOIL BETWEEN TREE ROOTS.** Soil pockets are easiest to find near the trunk of the tree, where roots have become stout and no longer riddle the earth. Just add some organic matter, as necessary, to get ground cover off to a good start, and then water as needed during dry weather.

Pocket plantings are great places to try less common and especially beautiful ground covers like European or American gingers, epimedium, and golden star.

289 USE LANDSCAPE FABRIC instead of plastic to reduce weeds in large plantings. Landscape fabric has pores that allow free air and water movement, a big advantage over impenetrable plastic. Lay it down before planting and then cut holes in the fabric. Plant your ground cover in the holes. When covered with mulch, landscape fabric, like plastic, prevents light from reaching the soil, which will stop the sprouting of most weed seeds.

290 HOLD BARREN SOIL IN PLACE WITH BURLAP when planting ground cover on a slope. This will prevent erosion while the ground cover is getting established. You should pin the burlap securely into the soil so that it won't slip off when rain makes the soil heavy and wet. Cut modest openings in the burlap and plant ground cover in each. Once the ground cover establishes a strong root system and is able to secure nearby soil from erosion, you can gradually enlarge the openings and allow it to spread until it fills out the slope.

291 SET GROUND COVER PLUGS IN PLACE USING A WIRE GRID

stretched over the bed for fast, easy planting. The regularly spaced openings will help you to coordinate spacing without need for a mea- suring tape (see Hint 211 for more information about spacing aids).

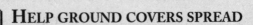

292 HELP GROUND COVERS SPREAD

by layering stems as they grow. Layering, a propagation method detailed in

Hint 109, encourages stems to root while still connected to the parent plant.

Ground covers such as pachysandra and periwinkle are easily rooted simply by covering barren portions of the stem with soil and keeping them moist. For harder-to-root ground covers like wintercreeper, you can remove a small piece of bark from the bottom of the stem and treat the opening with rooting hormone before covering the stem with soil.

293 **SPREAD NETTING OR OLD SHEETS OVER GROUND COVERS** during autumn leaf drop. It can be difficult to rake leaves out of thick ground covers, and allowing the leaves to sit and mat on the ground-cover bed creates unhealthy conditions. But planning ahead to catch leaves as they fall allows you to gather up all the leaves in one easy move and keeps the ground cover uncluttered.

294 REJUVENATE WINTER-BURNED GROUND-COVER PLANTINGS BY

MOWING. If a cold winter causes evergreens like ivy to grow brown and unsightly, don't give up hope. There is a good chance that the roots are still alive and will send up fresh green growth come springtime. Mowing off the old leaves gives the new leaves plenty of space and keeps the bed tidy.

CHAPTER 18

ROSES

The rose, one of the most glamorous garden flowers, continues to evolve into a more versatile part of the landscape. The earliest roses usually bloomed only once a year, but they gave off wonderful aromas. Old-fashioned roses can grow into large, thorny bushes, more vigorous than a modern hybrid tea rose.

In the early 1800s, reblooming roses from China were discovered and interbred with old-fashioned European roses to extend their bloom period. These hybrids had fewer thorns and petals but rebloomed through the summer. Breeding efforts focused on improving flower form and expanding color selection. The results were grandifloras, hybrid teas, and other long-blooming plants that required high maintenance.

Recently, to create hardier roses that need less spraying, have more fragrance, and bloom all summer, breeders began to infuse blood lines of the old-fashioned roses back into modern hybrids. This has created landscape roses, large or small bushes that bloom all season and have increased disease resistance. Many, but not all, are fragrant. They

CLASSIC OLD-FASHIONED ROSES

ALBA ROSES
'Semi Plena'
'Konigin von
   Danemark'

BOURBON ROSES
'Louise Odier'
'Variegata de
   Bologna'
'Madame Isaac
   Pereire'
'Honorine de
   Brabant'

CENTRIFOLIA ROSES
'De Meaux'

DAMASK ROSES
'Madame Hardy'
'Comte de
   Chambord'
'Celsiana'

GALLICA ROSES
Rosa gallica offici-
   nalis
'Cardinal de
   Richelieu'

MOSS ROSES
'Mundi'
'Empress Josephine'

are a wonderful way to enjoy the long-bloom beauty of the rose.

295 **CHOOSE SHRUB ROSES** over hybrid tea roses for low maintenance and disease resistance. Look for the following brands of high-quality shrub roses: David Austin English roses (from England), Town and Country Roses (from Denmark), Meidiland Romantica roses (from France), rugosa roses (developed from Oriental Rosa rugosa), and Explorer roses (extra-hardy hybrids from Ottawa Experiment Station in Canada).

296 **PROTECT A ROSE GRAFT,** the swollen knob near the base of the plant, from winter damage. Not all roses have grafts, but most hybrid teas, grandifloras, standard (tree form), and some miniatures are grafted. When planting, check for the graft and make arrangements to keep it from harm, if necessary. There are several options:

- In well-drained soil, you could plant the rose slightly deep, covering the graft with insulating soil. In cold climates, the graft union should be planted 2 to 3 inches below the soil line.

- Mound soil up over the graft in late fall and pull it back in spring.

- Surround the graft with shredded leaves, and hold the leaves in place with wire mesh.

- Buy plastic foam rose cones to cover the entire plant for extra insulation.

297 **TAKE GOOD CARE OF YOUR ROSES** so they will stay pest- and disease-resistant. Roses can be susceptible to a wide variety of problems, especially if they are growing weakly. Make sure they have well-drained, fertile soil. Water roses during dry weather and mulch them to conserve moisture. Prune to ensure each cane receives sun and good air circulation. With this kind of treatment, problems will be few and far between.

298 **PRUNE HYBRID TEAS, FLORIBUNDAS, AND OTHER ROSES** requiring heavy shaping back to 12 inches tall while they are dormant in spring. These roses flower on new growth, and nothing encourages new growth more than heavy spring pruning. While you are cutting stems back, take some time to remove any dead, diseased, or overcrowded canes. For shrub roses, pruning can be as simple as cutting out old and dead canes with long-handled pruning loppers.

299 **REMOVE ROOT SUCKERS** from grafted roses to keep them true. Many hybrid tea and floribunda roses are grafted on the extra-vigorous and disease-resistant roots of other species such as multiflora or rugosa roses. These root stocks may send up sprouts of their own, called suckers, which are easily identified by the different-looking foliage and flowers. Upon close inspection, you can see root suckers emerge from below the swollen graft. Clip suckers back as soon as you see them to keep the inferior sprouts from competing with your rose cultivar.

If the only sprouts that arise from the plant are off the roots, the graft has been damaged—which can occur during winter—and the original rose top is dead. If the root is a rugosa rose, you might try to grow it—it's a pretty plant. But if the root is a multiflora rose, it is a weed that is best taken out early.

300 **CONTROL BLACK SPOT** by planning ahead. Black spot, which marks leaves with black spots and then kills them, can spread up the plant and cause complete defoliation. Its damage is not pretty! But it can be avoided. Buy disease-resistant roses, including many of the landscape roses, polyantha roses such as 'The Fairy,' and even

---

IMPROVED CULTIVARS OF DISEASE-RESISTANT RUGOSA ROSES

'Blanc Double de Coubert'
'Fru Dagmar Hastrup'

'Linda Campbell'
'Topaz Jewel'
'Alba'

EASY-CARE POLYANTHAS

'The Fairy'   'Red Fairy'

---

disease-resistant hybrid tea roses like 'Olympiad.' Sprays with baking soda can prevent black spot infection. Even disease-resistant shrub roses can benefit from this in extra-humid or wet weather. See Hint 118 for directions.

Rake up and destroy any leaves infested with black spot. This helps eliminate spores that would otherwise reinfect healthy leaves.

301 **PLANT AROUND ROSE BUSHES** with low or medium-height fragrant herbs such as mints, sweet marjoram, oregano, thyme, bush basil, and German chamomile. These herbs provide an attractive cover for the barren bases of many roses and release an odor that can screen the plant from rose-eating pests. They will also provide a nice harvest for the kitchen. Forget about eating the herbs, however, if you spray the rose with chemicals unsuited for edible plants.

302 **LAYER RAMBLERS** and other roses to make new plants. Ramblers have long, limber canes that can be tied to a fence or trellis like a climbing rose. Notch the bark beneath the stem, remove nearby leaves, pin the stem to the ground, and mound over it with soil (see Hint 109).

Once rooted and cut free from the mother plant, you'll have a new plant growing on its own roots. It will have no need for graft protection!

303 **USE THE MINNESOTA TIP METHOD** in cold climates for winter protection of hybrid tea roses. In well-drained soil, dig a trench on one side of the rose. With your foot, gently push the rose canes into the trench, where they will be insulated underground. Mound soil over the canes and graft and mark the burial site with a stake so you can free the canes in early spring.

SHRUBS

While you may think of shrubs as "just bushes," they are actually much more. Shrubs come in a variety of shapes and sizes with many different types of foliage. Some shrubs produce berries, and others even provide fragrance! No matter what effect you are trying to achieve, there is undoubtedly a shrub that will fit the bill.

Creeping shrubs, like junipers, can serve as evergreen ground covers. Low, bushy shrubs like Japanese spirea and potentilla blend nicely into flower gardens or the front of a planting around the house. Larger, rounded shrubs can be grouped into clusters to define space or create privacy. More compact cultivars that mature when around 4 feet high, like 'Newport' viburnum, can be used around a house without any pruning. Taller shrubs, like Allegheny viburnum, are best kept at some distance from the house, where they won't block the views. They make good screens for the property perimeter. Vertical shrubs that are shaped like an upright cone or pillar, such as 'Skyrocket' juniper, create formality or emphasis in the yard. They can be striking when placed on either side of a doorway or garden gate.

Using a medley of shrub shapes offers design interest that goes much deeper than the leaves and flowers. And when you also take into account the other qualities shrubs have to offer, you'll see that they are an asset to any kind of garden.

304 **PLANT FRAGRANT FLOWERED SHRUBS** near doors or windows so you can enjoy their perfume both indoors and out.

305 CUT FLOWERING STEMS from your shrubs and bring them indoors to use in big bouquets. If you have large vases that dwarf ordinary annual or perennial stems, fill them with long branches of forsythia, lilacs, or viburnums. What a wonderful way to celebrate spring!

306 SLICE OFF CIRCLING OR TANGLED ROOTS before planting shrubs grown in

---

SOME SHRUBS WITH FRAGRANT FLOWERS

Butterfly bush

Blue spiraea

Summersweet

Fothergilla

Honeysuckle

Fantasy lilac

Dwarf Korean lilac

Miss Kim lilac

French lilac

Witch hazel

Burkwood viburnum

Fragrant snowball
   viburnum

Korean spice vibur-
num

---

containers. Potted shrubs fill the pot with roots, which then twine around and around. New roots may continue this destructive pattern even when planted if the old circling

roots are not removed. Eventually, the crown may be strangled by its own roots.

Use a pair of sharp pruning shears to slice off circling roots and loosen up matted roots. Releasing the healthy roots inside the root ball, planting the shrub in good soil, and keeping the area moist will encourage vigorous new root growth.

307 | SOAK THE ROOTS OF BARE-ROOT SHRUBS BEFORE PLANTING. Bare-root shrubs are dug in fall or spring, washed clean of soil, and shipped directly to mail-

order catalog customers. Shrubs commonly sold bare-root include Chinese abelia, bloodtwig dogwood, buttonbushes, viburnums, some forsythias, winterberry holly, and beauty bush, as well as hedge shrubs such as privet.

To ensure good results after planting, don't let the roots go into the soil dehydrated. An hour in a bucket of room-temperature water is all it takes. Plant immediately after soaking and keep moist through the entire first growing season.

308 **SCORE THE SIDES OF THE PLANTING HOLE** to encourage root penetration. In clay soils, slick-sided holes can dry to a glaze that is difficult for young roots to penetrate. Slicing into the hole perimeter with your shovel breaks up the glazing and creates openings where roots can burrow out.

309 **THIN OUT A THIRD TO HALF OF THE BRANCHES** of bare-root shrubs before planting. Your pruning shears will become one of your best planting tools, helping you put the shrub into a healthy balance before planting.

When shrubs are dug from the nursery field and processed for shipping, they lose most of their feeding roots, the delicate young roots responsible for absorbing moisture. Until the shrub is replanted and reestablishes new feeding roots, it can't support all the growth it once did. Pruning trims back shoots to balance root loss.

When pruning, begin by removing old, weak, damaged, or crowded branches at their base. But don't indiscriminately shear off the top of the plant. The terminal buds on the branch tips release hormones that encourage root growth and maintain a slow, orderly pattern of growth. These are both desirable qualities worth preserving in your shrubs.

310 **DEADHEAD HYBRID RHODODEN-DRONS AND MOUNTAIN LAURELS** to increase next year's bloom. Once the flowers begin to fade, use your thumb and forefinger (or pruning shears) to cut off the soft, immature flowering cluster. Just be careful not to damage nearby buds or shoots, which will soon be sprouting into new branches.

311 **CONSIDER CHANGING AN OVER-GROWN SHRUB** into a multi-stemmed tree. This works nicely with flowering plums, black haw viburnums, winged euonymus, and lilacs, all of which can grow to be 12 to 15 feet tall.

Begin by removing small, crowded upright stems to reveal a handful of shapely mature branches that can serve as trunks. Cut side shoots off the trunks up to about 5 feet off the ground, creating a tree form. Continue pruning as needed to keep the trunks clear of growth.

312 **WRAP BOXWOOD** and other evergreen shrubs with burlap to prevent winter burn. When the soil is frozen, the sun is bright, and wind is strong, evergreens lose moisture from their exposed leaves and cannot replace it through frozen roots. The foliage scorches to brown and the stems may die back—or even worse, the whole shrub may die. Burlap, although far from elegant, makes a neat coat for the shrub and ensures that you will have a nice-looking plant waiting for you when spring arrives. This also works for coniferous evergreens like arborvi-

SOME SHRUBS FOR SEASONAL BLOOMS

SPRING
Azaleas
Rhododendrons
Ornamental quince
Cotoneaster
Forsythia
Fothergilla
Lilac
Viburnum

SUMMER
Butterfly bush
Scotch heather

Blue spirea
Summersweet
Hydrangea
Rose-of-Sharon
St. John's wort
Potentilla
Spirea

FALL
Butterfly bush
Rose-of-Sharon
Witch hazel

tae. Be sure to water these shrubs well in the fall so they'll have plenty of moisture stored.

313 **BUILD A TEMPORARY WIRE FRAME** around tender shrubs—the species most likely to suffer winter damage in your area—and fill it with straw or leaves

for winter protection. Like
padding a carton of valu-
ables, this provides insulation from winter's worst
cold.

314 **DO NOT PLANT
BOXWOOD** and other brittle-stemmed
shrubs near the foundation of your house.
Heavy, wet, melting snow or chunks of ice
can slip off the roof and flatten shrubs resid-
ing below.

315 **PLANT SHRUBS THAT WILL
FLOWER IN SUCCESSION** through
the growing season. Get some spring, summer, and fall bloomers—then play them up,
using other plants as supporting characters.
Match the flower color of a viburnum with
a cluster of daffodils. Echo the color of a
rhododendron with a pot of pink pansies.

316 PLANT A CONIFEROUS SHRUB

GARDEN for winter fun. Use ever-greens with a variety of different shapes and leaf colors—gold, blue, gray, and green. In northern climates where winter is long, this kind of garden brightens the yard.

Suitable shrubs include dwarf firs, pines, hemlocks, spruces, heathers, junipers, arborvitaes, and false cypress. Specialty nurseries and catalogs abound with other, less common conifers as well. Interplant cone-shaped and vertical evergreens with low and mounded forms. Add in some spec-tacular weeping conifers for excitement, and contrast blue and gray foliage against green and gold. In summer, add some interplanted annuals, perennials, and ornamental grasses for variety.

FLOWERING TREES

Flowering trees can be one of the most memorable elements of the landscape. Fragrant flowering crabapples, frothy, aromatic fringe tree flowers, and weeping cherries dripping with pink blossoms can linger in the mind well after the flowers are gone.

For a lofty layer of flowers and greenery, flowering trees are magnificent when mixed with flowering shrubs, annuals, and perennials. But they are even more important in a yard with few flowers. Tree bark—silver, black, red, or green, either smooth or textured—can also be beautiful. Consider, for example, stewartia's peeling bark of gray, brown, orange, or red, as well as its creamy summer flowers and great fall color. The paper bark maple, with only small, early spring flowers, has glowing exfoliating, rust-colored bark and leaves that light up orange and red in fall. And colorful fall fruits provide a feast for the eyes as well as for the birds.

317 **CHOOSE TREES THAT HAVE WIDE CROTCH ANGLES** to avoid weak branches and ice damage. The crotch (or branch) angle measures the distance between the trunk and the base of the branch. An upright branch has a narrow crotch angle of less than 45 degrees. A sturdy, wide-angled branch has a 45- to 60-degree crotch angle.

The problem with branches that have narrow crotch angles, a common occurrence on trees like Bradford pears and plums, is that they are not well supported on the trunk. If coated with ice in a winter storm, they may split off. The narrow branching angle can also catch moisture and encourage diseases.

Another problem arises when upright-growing branches with narrow crotch angles near the top of a young tree begin to grow as fast as the main trunk. Prune the branches back to keep the trunk taller and dominant. If allowed to continue in this way, the tree develops a split leader, two trunks growing side by side. In severe weather, the trunks can crack apart, and the tree may be finished for good.

318 **USE SPREADERS ON YOUNG FRUIT TREES**
to correct narrow branch angles. Fruit trees are particularly prone to developing upright branches. Not only do these branches have all the problems mentioned in Hint 317, but they also grow tall and wild instead of

slowing down to flower and fruit. Shifting them into a more productive mode begins with creating a wider branch angle.

When the tree is young and flexible, you can prop short struts in the gap between a shoot and the trunk to force the branch down into a better 45-degree angle. Slightly older branches can be tied to a stake or weight to pull them down into position. Once the branches mature enough to become firm and woody, you can remove the spreaders, and the branches will stay in place.

319 **CHOOSE A FLOWERING TREE OVER A SHADE TREE** for a small garden. Not only is the size right—you'll also get beautiful flowers as a bonus.

- Trees that stay under 15 feet tall include 'Spring Glory' amelanchier, 'Crusader' hawthorn, and 'Camelot' crabapple.

SOME SMALLER FLOWERING TREES

Crabapples   Redbud
Hawthorns   Dogwoods
Yellowwood   Mountain ash
Palo verde   Tree lilacs
Flowering cherries Star magnolias and
Flowering plums   other magnolias

🌢 Trees that stay between 15 and 30 feet include 'Autumn Brilliance' amelanchier, redbuds, and kousa dogwoods.

320 **CHOOSE TREES THAT CAST LIGHT SHADE** if you want to plant a flower garden below them. Some trees allow sunlight to filter down between light branches or small leaves. Small, weeping, or long-trunked trees allow light to reach the flowers from the side during the morning and afternoon. Some good choices for mixed flower beds include crabapples, flowering plums, flowering cherries, franklin tree, golden chain tree, and Japanese tree lilac. Among the shade trees, consider honey locusts, ironwood, and birches.

321 AVOID PLANTING LARGE-FRUITED TREES OVER PATIOS AND DECKS.

Large crabapples, apples, pears, and other fruits and berries can mar the patio and

---

SOME CRABAPPLES WITH SMALL FRUIT

'American Masterpiece'	'Spring Snow' (no fruit)
'American Salute'	*'Camelot'
'Christmas Holly'	'Cankerberry'
'Donald Wyman'	*'Cinderella'
*'Louisa'	*'Excaliber'
M. sargentii	*'Guinevere'
'Weeping Candied Apple'	*'Lancelot'
	*'Snowdrift'

*Excellent choices for disease resistance

---

furniture, drop on people, and make steps slippery. Sweet, ripe fruit can attract yellow jackets and other critters. Let large fruits look pretty from afar, where they can drop unheeded in mulch, lawn, or ground cover. For outdoor living areas, choose tree cultivars with small or persistent fruit that won't drop and cause a mess.

322 **BUY FLOWERING TREES IN THE SPRING.** Trees purchased in the fall have probaby been sitting in the nursery lot all summer.

323 **PULL OR CUT OFF THE BURLAP BEFORE COVERING THE ROOTS WITH SOIL** when planting balled and burlapped stock. This simple bit of housekeeping can mean the difference between success and failure for the tree. Some trees are wrapped with synthetic burlap, which

will not decay and allow the roots to grow
free. Even
natural-fiber
burlap left
around the
roots can be slow to decay. It can wick mois-
ture away from the young roots, a sure way
to cause damage.

324 **CAREFULLY CONSIDER PLANTING
DEPTH** before digging the planting
hole for a new tree. You should make the
hole twice as wide but no deeper than the
root ball. Setting the ball on solid ground
that has not been fluffed by tilling or shoveling will provide a firm foundation. If the soil
underneath settles or shifts, the tree can sit
too deep.

If planting in heavy clay soil, you can
plant high so that the top third to half of the
root ball is above the soil surface. This allows

some roots to get up and out of soggy, poorly aerated soil. Fill in around the exposed roots with good soil, and top with mulch.

325 **CHECK THE ACCURACY OF YOUR PLANTING HOLE DEPTH** using a shovel handle. When you think the hole may be deep enough, set the root ball inside. Lay the shovel handle across the top of the hole. It should be even with or slightly lower than the top of the root ball.

326 **PLANT GROUPS OF FLOWERING TREES IN BEDS.** When growing in clusters or groves, flowering trees look spectacular in the landscape, much more so than isolated individual trees. There are other advantages to groupings:

- In poor soils, roots can grow freely through the entire amended bed.
- You can water and fertilize the entire group at the same time.
- The problem of mowing or trimming around the trunks is eliminated, saving time and damage to the bark.
- You can plant a shade garden in the grove.

327 **PLANT BENEATH YOUR TREES WITH GROUND COVERS** if you don't want a sea of mulch under them. Ground covers become a carpet of greenery and prevent mowing complications and root competition that can plague trees planted in turf.

CHAPTER 21

SHADE TREES AND EVERGREENS

Shade trees and evergreens are the
largest elements in the landscape, well
able to complement even the biggest
house. Use them to frame your home, but
plan ahead to ensure that the trees will not
become overwhelming; if you have a smaller
house, you should plant smaller trees than if
you have a very large home. With each passing year, big trees grow more valuable, increasing the worth of your house and property.

In winter, large trees have additional
benefits. The lofty greenery of a big pine,
spruce, or fir, or the dark, widespread limbs
of a handsome oak stand out amid a landscape of brown, white, and gray. Their very
stature demands respect, and in winter you
will have the luxury of enjoying them without rivalry.

But large trees do more than look elegant. Did you know that large trees can help lower your energy bills? Shade-casting trees to the south or west of your house can keep the house 10 degrees cooler in the summer. By starting some shade trees now, you are making an investment in the future.

328 CHOOSE PEST- OR DISEASE-RESISTANT SPECIES OR VARIETIES instead of problem-plagued trees. When you take the time to select a tree ideally suited for your site, your chances of long-term success are great. But they're even better when you check the track record of the tree you have in mind. If it's prone to insect or disease attack, continue your studies to find alternative, untroubled species or varieties. Because large shade trees can live for many years, spending an hour or two determining the best tree to plant will pay off.

Instead of European white birch, try disease-resistant river, 'Monarch,' or 'Avalanche' birches. A substitute for a silver maple tree is 'Celebration' maple. Try substituting 'Crusader' hawthorn for rust-susceptible hawthorns, and 'Metroshade' plane trees for disease-susceptible London plane trees.

329 **CHOOSE YOUNGER AND SMALLER TREES** to plant over larger ones. The motto "bigger is better" is not true in this case. Although you can have nearly full-sized trees planted in your yard (at a whopping price), smaller trees transplant more easily and grow more quickly than larger trees. They also cost less and are easier to handle without hiring landscapers.

It's best to start with a tree that has a 1- to 1½-inch trunk diameter (officially called its caliper). Very small seedlings—the kind given away by forestry departments on

Arbor Day—are a little too diminutive.
They take a long time to grow large enough
to be noticed in the yard, especially if hidden
amid grass.

330 **WHEN PLANTING FAST-GROWING TREES,** start with economical and quick-developing bare-root saplings. Fast-growing trees will increase in height by several feet a year. Under ideal conditions, a young tree that stands 3 feet tall upon planting will be up to 5, 6, or 7 feet tall the next year. The following year, it may be 10 feet tall or larger.

All trees require time to reach their prime, but fast growers stay on the move and hardly test your patience at all.

331 **LOOK TO SLOWER-GROWING TREES** for long, trouble-free lives and enough strength to withstand wind and ice storms.

FAST-GROWING TREES

Ash	Hackberry
Poplars	Red mulberry
Willows	Tulip tree
Arizona cypress	Cork tree
Eucalyptus	Japanese pagoda
Catalpa	tree
Honey locust	

SLOWER-GROWING TREES

Red maple	Pin oak
Sugar maple	English oak
Ginkgo	Pines
Sycamore	Spruces
White oak	Sourwood
Bur oak	Lindens

332 **INSPECT TREES FOR ANY GIRDLING ROOTS.** Just as a tight girdle can be oppressive to wear, girdling roots can squeeze a tree trunk and cut off its food supply.

Girdling roots are common on container-grown plants. It all begins when circling roots (see Hint 306) reach upward and loop around the bottom of the trunk. As the trunk grows wider, the roots cut into it and can strangle it. In less severe cases, girdling roots may only cut into one side of the tree, causing death of limbs serviced by the damaged wood.

If you inadvertently buy a tree with girdling roots, use your pruning shears to cut them off where they emerge from the crown before planting.

333 **CHECK TREES FOR DEEP ROOT COLLARS.** The root collar is the junction of roots and trunk, an important place that should be kept level with or above the soil surface when planting (see Hint 324).

Sometimes when nurseries cultivate between rows of field-grown trees and shrubs, extra soil may be thrown up above the roots and around the base of the trunk. When the root ball is dug up and wrapped in burlap, the bottom of the trunk (and the top of the roots) may actually be deep in the ball, with only barren soil above. This leaves the tree shortchanged on roots and the root collar unnaturally deep.

To test the depth of the root collar, rotate the trunk and see if it shifts deep in the ball, a sure sign of a deep root collar. Or, if the nursery will allow, pull back the burlap and brush back the soil to look for the junction of root and trunk.

334 **PLANT FAST-GROWING TREES** with slower-growing species to get shade fast. As the slower-growing trees get large enough to make an impact on the yard, cut out the weaker fast growers. You end up with the best of both worlds—quick greenery and lasting strength. See page 319 for a list of possible trees to plant.

335 **PLANT TREES IN A WIDE, SHALLOW HOLE,** at least twice the width of the root ball (see Hint 324). In the past, gardeners have been advised to plant trees in holes of many different shapes and sizes. But contemporary recommendations reflect new findings in how tree roots grow. Many trees concentrate their feeding roots in the top foot of soil. A wide hole loosens up an open, surface-hugging expanse for the early

growth of these roots and will help young trees get

established more quickly. There is no need to amend the soil—trees thrive best when they are established in native soil.

336 **SKIP STAKING** unless you are planting young trees in areas prone to strong winds. Staking can actually do more harm than good for young trees. If staked improperly, with rubbing or tight wires, the bark and trunk can become damaged, sometimes irreparably.

Staking also interferes with the natural movement of a tree swaying in the wind. Recent research has shown that swaying helps trees develop stronger, tapered trunks that will serve them well and keep them sturdy for decades.

Where staking is unavoidable, use flexible stakes and ties that have a couple inches of slack so the tree can continue to move. Pad the trunk or slip a section of rubber hose over the supporting wire so it won't damage the tree. Remove the stakes as soon as the tree has rooted enough to become self-supporting.

337 **WRAP THE TRUNK OF THIN-BARKED TREES,** most notably fruit trees, in winter to help keep the bark from splitting. Tree wraps and firmer plastic tree guards can also discourage rabbits and rodents from chewing on the bark and can prevent accidental damage from mowers.

Remove the tree wrap in the spring so it won't get too tight on the swelling trunk or provide a hiding place for pests.

338 **ADJUST HOW YOU WATER A YOUNG TREE** as it gets established.

When it is first planted and for the following growing season, provide water directly on the planting site. You can allow a hose to trickle gently over the root ball, making a shallow saucer of soil below the leafy canopy to keep the water from running off (see Hint 29).

Once the tree has established enough new roots to grow vigorously, use soaker hoses to water just outside the perimeter of the tree canopy. This will encourage the roots to spread outward, providing a stronger foundation for the tree.

339 **MULCH THE TREE PROPERLY.** Put a layer of bark mulch, wood chips, or compost from the drip line (below the perimeter of the branch canopy) to 4 inches from the trunk (not too close or problems can arise).

Mulching will help eliminate weeds and keep the planting site moist. It also looks good and gives the landscape a polished feel.

Avoid excessively thick layers of mulch, which can limit soil aeration in heavy ground and cause roots to smother. Another problem occurs when thick heaps of mulch break down into rich organic matter. Shallow-rooted trees like maples can grow thick root mats in the mulch (which is not good), and some of those roots may start to girdle (which is even worse!—see Hint 332). Shallow roots are also subject to excessive drying in summer.

340 **PLANT EVERGREENS IN SPRING OR SUMMER** up to about mid-August, but no later. To support their foliage through winter, they need to have a well-established root system and plenty of internal moisture before the ground freezes.

341 AVOID PLANTING TREES THAT DEER ESPECIALLY ENJOY EATING where deer are abundant. Some of their favorites include yews, arborvitaes, and some pines. Concentrate instead on some of their least favorite trees, including maples, beech, ashes, ginkgo, honey locust, tulip tree, sour gum, spruce, sycamore, oaks, willows, and bald cypress.

342 HELP PREPARE EVERGREEN TREES FOR DRY WINTER WEATHER by watering them more in the fall, especially when rainfall has been limited. It's also helpful to spray leaves with an antitranspirant coating, which limits evaporation from the foliage.

343 DON'T PLANT SALT-SUSCEPTIBLE EVERGREENS NEAR THE STREET in cold climates. Salt used for snow and ice control will splash up on the needles and drip into the soil. It won't be long before a thriving tree begins to brown out and then fail. Look for trees that can withstand salt spray. An example of a salt-susceptible evergreen is white pine. Some other possibilities include sycamore maple, shadblow, Austrian black pine, Japanese black pine, Red mulberry, and sour gum.

344 **ENJOY A TREE THAT CAN DOUBLE AS A SCULPTURE** by planting a curly-limbed willow. Twisted branches and curling leaves make interesting focal points on small willows such as 'Golden Curls' and 'Scarlet Curls.'

345 **PREVENT SUMMER SPIDER MITE ATTACKS** on your evergreens by spraying susceptible plants with a hose every day during hot, dry weather. If you're out watering the garden, turn the hose on the evergreen foliage as well. Water helps to dislodge spider mites and discourage their multiplication, a great nontoxic preventative.

346 **ADD AN UPRIGHT ACCENT IN NARROW SPACES** (such as courtyard gardens) with special, extra-slender trees. Some examples are 'Columnaris' European hornbeam, 'Dawyck' European beech, 'Princeton Sentry' ginkgo, and 'Columnaris' Swiss stone pine.

347 **ADD SPICE TO THE LANDSCAPE** by growing peacocks, which are trees with uniquely colored foliage held all season long. Some of the choices that you might consider are red-leaved Japanese maples, golden-leaved box elders and tulip trees, or purple-leaved Norway maples and beech trees.

Some trees with colorful foliage are

commonly available at garden centers and nurseries. Others can be found at specialty nurseries.

348 **INCLUDE SOME SHADE TREES WITH BOLD FALL COLOR** for an exciting finish to the growing season. As autumn approaches, trees begin breaking down green chlorophyll and storing the components away for winter. This reveals underlying leaf coloration, which was there all along but hidden beneath the green pigments.

Among the best trees for fall color are maples, birches, sourwood, ginkgo, tulip tree, red oak, linden, and white ash such as 'Autumn Applause,' all of which are outstanding when nights are cool and days are sunny.

CHAPTER 22

CONTAINERS

Containers are an excellent way to learn about gardening because they're easy to plant and give great results quickly. They also provide color to highlight patios, steps, garden gates, or anywhere else you find to be a little drab. In addition, pots are the best places to show off rare and exotic plants.

Containers eliminate much of the guesswork in gardening. There is no need to tolerate difficult soil or make do with marginal sites. You can start with any potting mix, picking the perfect blend for the plants you want to grow. You can set the pot where it will have the ideal amount of sun or shade. You provide water when nature comes up short, and you schedule the fertilization. There is nothing left to chance, assuming of course that you take the time to tend the potted plant.

In return, containers become living flower arrangements. With lively color schemes, varied textures, and handsome containers, potted plants grow, flower, and flourish close at hand where they are easily enjoyed.

349 **PLANT ANNUALS IN A BIG BAG OF POTTING SOIL** for a quick, easy balcony garden. This method, commonly used in England, is still a novelty here and will make a great conversation piece:

- Lay the bag flat on the ground where you want a mini garden. Punch a few small drainage holes in the bottom.
- You can cut one large opening in the top side

for several plants, letting them inter-
mingle in a decorative planting scheme.
Or make several individual planting
holes for a working garden of annual
vegetables and herbs.

🍃 The plastic wrapper will help to keep
the soil inside moist. But when it does
begin to dry out, or needs water-soluble
fertilizer as a plant pick-me-up, carefully
drizzle water or water-soluble fertilizer
inside to moisten the entire bag.

350 **USE CARE WHEN PLANTING IN
DECORATIVE CONTAINERS.** Lovely
bark, wicker, wood, and even fine pottery
pots and urns make handsome containers.
But some of them have one big drawback—
they can be damaged by water. Regardless,
you can still use them for plants, but only as
an ornamental cover over a working pot
below. Here is the trick:

- Plant in a plastic pot that has no drainage holes or that sits on a plastic saucer, which will prevent moisture spills.

- The pot, and saucer if used, must be smaller than the decorative container.

- Put a layer of plastic inside the container, then set the potted plant on top.

- Cover the top of the pots with sheet

MATERIALS FOR CONTAINERS	
Plastic	Stone
Clay	Cement
Ceramic	Cedar
Fiberglass	Redwood
Brass	Compressed fibers
Bronze	Compressed peat
Tin	moss

moss or other natural fibers to hide the mechanics below.

This combination will be temporary at best and require careful watering so the plant roots won't be drowned or dried. Once every couple of months, remove the potted plant and water thoroughly, draining off the excess moisture to wash out salts that will build up in the soil.

351 **STERILIZE OLD POTS** with a 10 percent bleach solution before using them for other plants. Saving old pots from flowers, vegetables, poinsettias, even shrubs transplanted into the yard is a great way to economize. But you have to be certain to eliminate any disease spores that may have come, like extra baggage, with the previous occupant.

Begin by washing out excess soil, bits of roots, and other debris with warm soapy water. Mix 1 part household bleach with 9 parts water and use the solution to wipe out the pot. Rinse again, and the pot is ready to plant.

352 CREATE YOUR OWN CUSTOM POTTING SOIL. Use a peat-moss-based potting mix as the foundation. (It works well for houseplants, seedlings, and many other plants as is.) Peat-based mixes won't compress like true soil, which is a big advantage in pots. But they are low on nutrients and liable to dry out quickly, complications that can be minimized with special potting blends.

- To make a richer mix for annual flowers or for perennials like daylilies, you can blend 2 parts peat mix with 1 part compost.

- For a more fertile, moisture-retentive soil for tomatoes or lettuce, blend 1 part peat mix, 1 part garden soil, and 1 part compost.

🌿 For a lighter mix for propagating cuttings or growing succulents or cacti, add 1 part coarse sand or perlite to 1 part peat mix.

353 PREMIX A WHEELBARROW FULL OF POTTING BLEND (see Hint 352).

If you have plenty of houseplants that need repotting, or you like to put more than just a few pots or window boxes of summer flowers outdoors, this will save you time and effort. And if you buy the peat mix and extras in large, economy-sized bags, it also will save you money.

354 **PREMOISTEN PEAT-BASED MIXES** in a large tub or wheelbarrow. Prewetting peat moss, which soaks up a surprisingly large amount of water, ensures there will be enough moisture left over to supply new plantings.

Premoistening is easily done with a garden hose. Sprinkle in a generous amount of water, and work the moisture into the peat mix with a trowel (or a hoe if you are making large batches). Continue to add more water until the peat clumps together in a moist ball. Then it is ready to go in a pot.

355 **PLACE A CIRCLE OF FINE MESH SCREEN OVER POT DRAINAGE HOLES** instead of using pebbles or pot shards. The screen will help to hold the soil in place until the roots fill out and claim every particle. But it's still a good idea to water outdoors, in the sink, or over a pot saucer so a little oozing dampness or soil won't damage anything.

The problem with covering drainage holes with pot shards (the clay chunks left after a pot is broken) and pebbles is that they can shift to clog up the drainage holes. With no place for excess water to go, plant roots may soak in saturated soil, a condition few plants emerge from alive.

356 USE WATER-HOLDING GELS to reduce the need for watering, especially when planting in quick-drying, peat-based mixes. These gels—actually polymers—look like crystals when dry and safely sealed in their package. But once you add water, you'll be surprised to see them swell up into a large mass of quivering gelatin look-alikes. You can blend the gel into potting mixes, following blending instructions on the package.

357 **USE WINDOW BOXES** to brighten your house with flowers and add height to surrounding gardens.

- Elegant window boxes can feature vibrant flowers that match the color of nearby curtains, carpets, shrubs, or shutters.

- Some cascading ivy, vinca vine, or vining petunias will soften the geometric outlines of the window box.

- Grow herbs such as thyme, basil, and parsley in a kitchen window box.

358 **SET A NARROW PERFORATED** pvc pipe in the center of a strawberry pot or large container before filling in around it with potting mix. When you need to water your plants, run the hose gently into the

pipe, and the water will ooze out from top to bottom, inside to outside, giving every plant an even share.

359 **USE SLOW-RELEASE FERTILIZERS** to keep plants growing and blooming all season. Because peat-based mixes contain little or no natural nutrients, plant growth depends on a regular supply of fertilizer. Slow-release fertilizers keep working for several months to a year, depending on the formulation.

360 **SEAL THE BOTTOMS OF CLAY SAUCERS WITH POLYURETHANE** to keep them watertight. Then they will be safe to use on floors and carpets. Or, instead of buying clay saucers, you can buy watertight plastic saucers made to look like clay. When one is sitting beneath a pot, it's hard to tell the difference.

361 **KEEP A SUCCESSION OF NEW FLOWERS BLOOMING** in pots throughout the seasons, so your home and yard will never be short on color.

- In spring, enjoy cool-season flowers like forced bulbs (see Hint 259), primroses, and pansies.
- In summer, grow tender perennials and annuals like impatiens and begonias.

FOLIAGE PLANTS for CONTAINERS

These plants look great when they're mixed with flowering plants in pots.

Caladiums	Hostas
Croton	Scented geraniums
Ferns	Artemisias
Asparagus fern	Spider plants
Rex begonias	Ivies

❧ In fall, enjoy late bloomers like asters and mums.

362 **PUT CLAY AND PLASTIC POTS IN THE GARAGE** before cold winter weather arrives. This will help keep them from cracking and chipping when the weather turns bitterly cold.

363 **WRAP HEAVY URNS AND POTS** that are too bulky to carry indoors in plastic for winter protection. Do this on a dry autumn day, securing the plastic across the top, bottom, and sides of the pots to prevent moisture from getting inside. Moisture expands when it freezes. This causes terracotta, ceramic, and even synthetic stone and concrete containers to chip and break.

364 **STORE POTS UNDER TARP** for protection in mild climates. This will save space in your garage or basement and keep the pots handy for when you need them in the spring.

365 **LOOK FOR SELF-WATERING** planters if you aren't home enough to keep potted plants from drying out (or if you forget to water every day or two). Self-watering planters have a water reservoir in the bottom that's connected to the pot by a water-absorbing wick. When the soil begins to get dry, the wick pulls up more water from the reservoir.

INDEX